BUILDING ON WHOLE LEADERSHIP

Energizing and Strengthening Your Early Childhood Program

Marie Masterson, PhD
Michael Abel, PhD
Teri Talan, EdD, JD
Jill Bella, EdD

Gryphon House
www.gryphonhouse.com

Published by Gryphon House, Inc.
P. O. Box 10, Lewisville, NC 27023
800.638.0928; 877.638.7576 (fax)
Visit us on the web at www.gryphonhouse.com.

Library of Congress Cataloging-in-Publication Data
The cataloging-in-publication data is registered with the Library of Congress for ISBN 978-0-87659-824-5.

Bulk Purchase
Gryphon House books are available for special premiums and sales promotions as well as for fund-raising use. Special editions or book excerpts also can be created to specifications. For details, call 800.638.0928.

Disclaimer
Gryphon House, Inc., cannot be held responsible for damage, mishap, or injury incurred during the use of or because of activities in this book. Appropriate and reasonable caution and adult supervision of children involved in activities and corresponding to the age and capability of each child involved are recommended at all times. Do not leave children unattended at any time. Observe safety and caution at all times.

Table of Contents

Introduction   1

Chapter 1:
Understanding Your Influence as a Leader   5

Chapter 2:
Building a Foundation: Leadership Essentials   16

Chapter 3:
Applying the Tools of Leadership Essentials   36

Chapter 4:
Maximizing Pedagogical Leadership   58

Chapter 5:
Using Tools for Pedagogical Leadership   79

Chapter 6:
Encouraging Family Engagement   93

Chapter 7:
Advancing Administrative Leadership   107

Chapter 8:
Applying Tools for Effective Administrative Leadership   121

Chapter 9:
Leveraging Your Leadership Qualities   132

References and Recommended Reading   150

Index   167

Acknowledgments

We want to acknowledge the deep investment of the Whole Leadership Committee at the McCormick Center for Early Childhood Leadership. The committee worked to develop the framework and gave their ongoing support to refine it. Thank you to Giovanni Arroyo, Marleen Barrett, Melissa Casteel, Sonja Crum-Knight, Lindsey Engelhardt, Safiyah Jackson, Tarah Kadzielawski, and Barb Volpe. We are also grateful to the McCormick Center Advisory Board for their focused discussion and feedback and to the hundreds of early childhood professionals who contributed to the development of the Whole Leadership Framework through the McCormick Center blog series, in workshop sessions at the Leadership Connections conference, and through individual communication.

Introduction

If you are an early childhood program leader, this book is for you. In a single day, you manage operations, build relationships with families, oversee teaching, and plan professional development. You are an expert in child development, child guidance, licensing standards, and policy. With all of these pressing responsibilities, how can you foster a stronger sense of purpose and collaboration in your program? How do you balance priorities? How will you accomplish your goals while maintaining perspective and energy?

The Whole Leadership Framework offers an opportunity for you to refresh your sense of purpose, energize your practice, and focus on the most important ingredients of leadership success. In this book, you will find useful tools and resources to help you balance your priorities and effectively lead your program. The framework will help you develop a cohesive, sustainable, and vibrant organization.

Where Did the Whole Leadership Framework Originate?

Transforming the Workforce for Children Birth through Age 8: A Unifying Foundation (Institute of Medicine and National Research Council 2015) introduced a mandate to strengthen the capacity of early childhood program leaders. Leaders needed common language, clearly defined priorities, and cohesive direction to support professional development and set goals for program success. To clarify direction for the field and to give support for the internal growth and effectiveness of programs a unified framework was needed.

The Whole Leadership Framework, developed through the work of the McCormick Center for Early Childhood Leadership, addresses this gap and introduces an integrated and holistic way to revitalize the work of early childhood leaders.

The framework emerged from engagement among early childhood leaders around the United States and within the McCormick Center. Incorporating feedback from early childhood leaders across sectors, the framework was refined to focus on the most important ingredients of leadership success: leadership essentials, pedagogical leadership, and administrative leadership. The model introduces balance across domains, creates integrated connections among the domains, and illustrates the priorities of all types of early care and education program models serving children from birth through third grade.

What Is the Whole Leadership Framework?

The interdependent relationships among leadership essentials, pedagogical leadership, and administrative leadership ensure the health and success of programs. As the framework demonstrates, the program leader functions as a facilitator for the overall vision, direction, and daily management of an early childhood program. This leader has the authority to delegate some leadership functions to others in an organization and to coordinate tasks to ensure that goals are met. The Whole Leadership Framework creates a model to do this effectively.

- **Leadership essentials** includes the basic competencies and individual qualities that are foundational to the effectiveness of all facets of leadership. Essentials include competencies in self-awareness, communication, and relationship building, characteristics that shape the dynamics and interpersonal systems of your program. Leadership essentials affect all aspects of pedagogical and administrative leadership.

- **Pedagogical leadership** supports teaching and learning. While discussions about teaching usually focus on what teachers do in classrooms, pedagogical leadership provides a more complete foundation that includes competency in early childhood development and teaching knowledge. Pedagogy includes the program philosophy, the physical environment and materials, routines, activities, and interactions that influence teaching quality. This dimension also addresses the program leader's role in selecting curriculum, overseeing teacher qualifications, ensuring ongoing feedback and support for teaching staff, facilitating professional development opportunities, and building communities of practice to ensure continuous quality improvement. In addition, pedagogical leadership includes promotion of family engagement and work with families.

- **Administrative leadership** keeps a program stable and facilitates growth through maximizing the team's capacity to develop and sustain a vital early childhood organization. It incorporates operational and strategic leadership functions, including creating program policies, developing systems for efficient operation, ensuring organizational supports for effective teaching, managing budgets and funding, and overseeing building and personnel needs. Administrative leadership includes both leadership and management functions in the organization. As a program leader, you set the strategic direction for the program and also assume various leadership roles beyond your own organization. Through advocacy and connecting with your communities and its resources, you expand the scope of your influence and effectiveness.

Leadership is the most important stabilizer, shaping how your program functions. It is essential to the organizational health and efficacy of program effectiveness for staff, families, and children. Instead of approaching each part of your work separately, the Whole Leadership Framework offers the opportunity to use an integrated and holistic approach that will strengthen all aspects of your work. Importantly, the framework will increase your influence as a professional and provide the tools and resources you need to increase your productivity within and outside your organization.

Whole Leadership Framework
FOR EARLY CHILDHOOD PROGRAMS (BIRTH TO THIRD GRADE)

PEDAGOGIAL LEADERSHIP

Leading the art and science of teaching with an emphasis on educator dispositions and high-quality interactions with children. This includes ensuring fidelity to curricular philosophy, assessing children's development and learning, using data for evaluation, and optimizing learning environments.

- **Instructional leadership:** Supporting educators in implementing curriculum

- **Family engagement:** Promoting partnerships with families and fostering family leadership

ADMINISTRATIVE LEADERSHIP

Coordinating work and mobilizing people to ensure the organization remains stable and continues to grow.

- **Operational leadership:** Ensuring adequate equipment and space, guiding the development and management of budgets, fostering a positive workplace, and hiring and supporting staff

- **Strategic leadership:** Goal setting and guiding future program direction

- **Advocacy leadership:** Acting as an ambassador for the needs of children, families, and programs

- **Community leadership:** Collaborating with organizations within the local community on behalf of the children and families served

WHOLE LEADERSHIP

is an **interdependent relationship** that exists among leadership domains. A **balanced perspective** is necessary when performing administrative functions.

LEADERSHIP ESSENTIALS

Foundational competencies and individual qualities necessary for leading people that are expressed in personal leadership styles and dispositions. Leadership essentials are often developed through reflective practice.

Personal Attributes:

- Self-efficacy
- Empathy
- Creativity
- Authenticity
- Humility
- Transparency
- Adaptability
- Learning

Source: McCormick Center for Early Childhood Leadership. 2019. Whole Leadership Framework. Wheeling, IL: McCormick Center for Early Childhood Leadership. Used with permission.

The Whole Leadership Framework provides common language for communication with staff, coaches, and policy professionals as you address, support, and advance the needs of young children, families, and staff. As you face a long "to-do" list and prioritize a range of significant obligations, you will be able to make critical decisions about how to balance your time, energy, and priorities for the most productive results. The visual and conceptual roadmap will help you integrate each function of your work more effectively into the context of your whole organization and its goals.

How This Book Is Organized

The content and features of this book show you how to use the Whole Leadership Framework to identify the strengths, capabilities, and needs of your organization. You will find practical strategies to create action steps to make the most of growth opportunities. In addition to new ideas for daily practice, you will benefit from real-life scenarios and reflections from other professionals that provide insight about how to achieve greater effectiveness, cohesion, and impact.

This book invites program leaders to use the framework to identify the strengths and capabilities of their organization and to take practical steps to engage in meaningful professional growth. The features will inspire and encourage you to take positive steps in your leadership journey.

- **Real-Life Scenarios:** Each section uses vignettes showing benefits, lessons learned, and the ways the book's content affects and supports leaders.

- **Legacies of Leadership:** This feature, indicated by 🔑, provides tips, success stories, and inspirational quotes from leaders that show how the principles and practices of whole leadership can make a difference in your organization. These examples represent the combined wisdom of program administrators and are not attributed to any one particular speaker.

- **What Works Best:** Indicated by ⚙️, these brief research-to-practice information boxes highlight the latest evidence-based knowledge about what works to anchor your leadership practice.

- **Take-Away Strategies:** These practical application steps, indicated by 🖼️, provide an on-the-spot opportunity to integrate content into your daily work.

- **Digging Deeper:** These brief resource sections, indicated by 🛠️, provide additional information for readers to pursue a topic in depth.

- **Chapter Study Guides:** At the end of each chapter, guiding questions and activities frame active reflective evaluation and planning. The study guide can be used individually for self-study or to facilitate a group study within a community of practice for program leaders. Study guides may be copied.

As you read each chapter, you will discover practical information and strategies to help you overcome barriers to effective planning and practice. You will become part of a national initiative that strengthens and prioritizes the influence of early childhood leaders in guiding continuous quality-improvement efforts. The Whole Leadership Framework will help you maximize your impact as a change agent in the lives of children, families, organizations, and communities.

Understanding Your Influence as a Leader
Unpacking the Challenges and Opportunities of Leadership

Program director Allyeah wants to encourage effective planning. She has asked teachers for ideas about strengthening relationships with families. She hopes to encourage individual effort and at the same time support cohesive program goals. Inviting teachers to brainstorm has been a productive way to build confidence and incorporate staff ideas to promote family collaboration.

Teachers Samina and Jasmine brainstorm strategies to connect with families. Samina says, "I want to use puppet play to teach social skills." Jasmine adds, "Maybe we can ask parents to teach manners at home." Allyeah encourages them. "I'll include a weekly manners tip in the newsletter. Each of these strategies will help us reach our goals."

A leader's responsibilities can be overwhelming. On a day-to-day basis, program leaders need to clarify goals, motivate staff, foster organizational norms and expectations, and ensure teachers have needed resources for success. But these priorities often take a back seat to the daily management of the program—maintaining adequate funding, meeting multiple reporting requirements, and participating in quality-improvement efforts. Responding to the needs of children and families (or substituting in the classroom) may require time that conflicts with planning and preparation for staff growth and development.

Time management is a pressing challenge. Scheduling required meetings, creating effective daily routines, and managing communication about changes to families' schedules all require attention and time. Policies that appear to be clear in a handbook may be missed, misunderstood, or questioned. Making phone calls and following up on email communication can require more time than expected.

Daily challenges may feel overwhelming when teachers are unexpectedly absent and temporary substitutes need to be secured. At times you are needed in a classroom to maintain ratio or to manage staffing breaks and schedules. Time on the phone with a temporary staffing agency, hiring an extra teacher, and managing the budget for capacity coverage can interfere with other priorities. The need to find and hire strong staff, along with ongoing changes in external licensing, state standards, and assessment requirements, can be daunting.

⚙️ What Works Best: Exploring Primary Challenges

Primary challenges for program leaders include making leadership visible and valued, assuring positive outcomes for children, and managing change (Coleman et al. 2016). Leaders need to mandate formal organizational structures and ensure clear roles for staff, yet at the same time foster relationships and a collaborative learning environment (Colmer et al. 2014). The functions of leadership and management need to be integrated in a cohesive way so staff can accomplish what is necessary in a timely and efficient way, yet the program leader needs to mobilize others to take on those challenges as their own (Hay 2012).

Conflicts between daily realities and the needs of individual staff can interfere with program cohesion and goals (Nuttall et al. 2018). In addition to internal demands, external requirements such as standards, accountability, and external systems may conflict with internal priorities such as intentional teaching, strength-based mindsets, cultural responsiveness, collaboration, and organizational identity (Carter 2016). The Whole Leadership Framework can unify organizational vision and help balance internal and external resources critical to meet the needs of children and families (Abel et al. 2017).

🖼️ Take-Away Strategies: Making Time for Overall Goals

In planning for the complex needs of an early childhood program, your ability to manage time, priorities, and planning is essential. You may need to get organized but can't seem to get out from under pressing needs long enough to feel proactive. You may need to evaluate what is working well and identify what needs to change. As you examine the priorities and the goals of your program, make sure your basic organizational approaches are in place:

- **Keep your vision clear.** Define the specific goals you want to achieve. Do your goals inform your decisions, motivate your efforts, and drive your plans?
- **Get organized.** Set aside an hour or more each week for calendar updates and planning.
- **Keep a time log.** Track how much time you spend on specific areas of work. Use this information to allocate time for tasks and plan realistic timeframes for projects.
- **Arrange your information.** Create a working system for storage of records, frequently needed information, and file management so that you conserve time for important priorities.
- **Write a plan for future success.** Take time to evaluate what is not working well. Don't do the same thing tomorrow yet expect different results. When frustrations arise, be your own best coach.
- **Evaluate what happened.** Write action steps to keep yourself on track the next time you encounter the same challenge.

Anchoring Your Work in the Whole Leadership Approach

Claretta finally has a minute to return to her office after lunch just as the phone rings. It is Libby, the chairperson of the community early literacy workgroup. "Claretta, you are just the person I am looking for. Would you be able to serve on the budget committee? We meet once a month on Thursday night at the library."

Claretta pauses. "I really want to, but I need to think about whether I can fit it in. May I call you back and let you know?"

Libby replies, "Okay. But you know we need you."

Like many directors, Claretta works at maximum capacity. She feels as if she is in over her head and needs to weigh her energy and resources. She is determined to keep her life in balance and is struggling to manage her schedule. With many demands, she knows she has to postpone saying yes until she has time to evaluate the rest of her schedule and priorities. In the morning, she calls Libby to suggest another director who might be a good match.

Often a day brings a barrage of unexpected events, people, and circumstances. You may begin the day with a well-planned to-do list but find that, at five o'clock, you haven't begun to tackle what you thought were your priorities. At times it can feel like trying to put together a thousand-piece puzzle without a picture on the box cover to guide your choices. You work on a small section, begin to feel discouraged, and randomly shift to a new color or pattern. You make gradual progress, but don't have a sense about how the sections will fit together.

In the same way, having a visual picture of whole leadership can help you sort your priorities, decide where to focus your attention, and better understand how the pieces in one part of the puzzle affect other parts. With a picture of the whole, you will more quickly recognize when a piece is missing and when you need to pay attention to subtle patterns. With a visual guide, you will more quickly understand how leadership areas fit together, notice when you have overlooked an obvious need, and adjust to keep your organization on track toward clear goals.

Use the Whole Leadership Framework as a visual roadmap to help you plan in proactive and intentional ways for challenges and be able to step out with greater confidence to lead positive change. Rather than considering leadership and management, professional learning, and working with families as separate silos, integrate your work to strengthen your ability to evaluate and plan. You can use the Whole Leadership Framework to make connections from the work itself to the outcomes you want to achieve.

As you think about organizational planning and goal setting, leadership essentials will help you evaluate and strengthen your own skills as you build the capacity of your staff. While strengthening your program's philosophy and teaching approaches, pedagogical leadership will help you make the most of your environment, approaches to teaching, classroom interactions, and family engagement. As you manage the operational and strategic functions of your program, administrative leadership will help you create efficiencies, and expand your effectiveness and influence.

Exploring the dimensions of the Whole Leadership Framework in detail will help you to better understand how to evaluate the various requirements and challenges of your work. What previously seemed like an unrelated issue will soon seem connected to a more cohesive whole. You will be able to allocate your time, energy, and planning to manage and innovate your work. The framework will help you communicate priorities and goals to engage staff, families, and others who participate in and support your program.

⚙ What Works Best: Strengthening the Influence of the Program Administrator

What aspects of your program require time, effort, and planning? As you consider your priorities as a program leader, you may find that you are responsible for the following:

- You establish and maintain program norms and ensure a positive organizational climate and an integrated, collaborative culture (Ostroff, Kinicki, and Muhammad 2013). As a vital role model, you inspire others to understand and commit to common goals. You hire and train staff and plan to help them thrive and grow within your organizational philosophy and mission.

- You facilitate quality-improvement efforts (Lieberman 2017). You foster reflective practice and plan professional-development training to create positive change (Ang 2012). You facilitate conversations with staff to define program strengths and identify areas that need improvement. With successive cycles of evaluation, you implement new approaches, reflect with staff about progress made, and integrate additional action steps.

- You ensure staff use developmentally appropriate and culturally responsive practice (Bloom 2014; Minkos et al. 2017). You facilitate staff reflection about the ways culture is integrated with learning and encourage teaching and communication that is congruent with linguistic, family, and community contexts.

- You cultivate commitment among staff to nurture family and community partnerships (Derman-Sparks et al. 2015). You set aside time to facilitate learning with staff about the role of families and identify strategies to foster family engagement.

- You manage business and organizational aspects of program administration and recognize their impact on the quality of the learning environment (Dennis and O'Connor 2013; Talan et al. 2014). You fine-tune administrative functions to ensure viable systems to carry out the program mission.

- You act as liaison between the program, community, and early childhood system to ensure all elements of the program operate as a whole to promote optimal results for children and families (ECSWG 2014; Tout et al. 2015). These linkages garner needed connections for early intervention, provide information to families about needed services, foster successful transitions to school, and strengthen professional supports for the program and those it serves.

Leading with a Whole-Child, Whole-Person Mindset

The program director, Jacquie, holds family meetings three times each year. The events are held at the end of the program day, and child care is provided. As families arrive, they find handouts and resources on a variety of topics, such as local educational opportunities, nutrition guidelines, health brochures, parenting and positive-guidance tips, and flyers highlighting local art and music events for children. This month, the presenters are discussing sleep challenges. The session is packed.

The event begins with a greeting by Jacquie, followed by a presentation by a community child-development specialist and a pediatrician. Pediatrician Dr. Hayworth addresses the attentive group: "It's hard raising a child. You have to balance your child's needs with your own. In many cases, your child's needs keep you from meeting your own—like when your child wakes up in the night or is sick. Let's talk about what you can do to make bedtime, naptime, and sleep routines work for you."

After the brief presentation, the presenters respond to specific questions about personal experiences.

Jacquie and her team have embraced the principles of child-centered practice. They know that children are affected by personal, family, community, social, and policy factors that foster resilience and healthy development. They weigh daily decisions in the program by keeping in mind the best interests of the children and families they serve. They partner with community organizations that share their values and connect families to resources that can strengthen the quality of life for children. This is the foundational philosophy of the organization.

⛏ Digging Deeper: Trauma-Informed Care

In addition to knowledge of high-quality teaching and responsive nurturing, staff should be aware of the effects of stress on children and families. Children who have experienced early stress or trauma benefit especially from safe, predictable routines. Attentive and secure relationships strengthen emotion regulation and instill trust and security. Staff can learn about trauma-informed teaching and use strategies that help children monitor and mediate stress. As the program director, you can facilitate wellness initiatives. Make materials available that connect families to community mental-health resources. For more information about trauma-informed teaching and care, see chapter 6. In addition, explore the United States Department of Health and Human Services Administration for Children and Families resources and links: https://www.acf.hhs.gov/trauma-toolkit/schools

---

The components of the whole-child, whole-school, whole-community model ensure all foundations for success are fully integrated in school-based settings (Centers for Disease Control and Prevention 2018). In the same way, the Whole Leadership Framework integrates all elements of leadership that support the effectiveness of a program. The goal is to provide the highest quality setting and strengthen families as full partners in children's education and development. Whole leadership focuses on all aspects of program vitality, including staff motivation; cultural foundations; and the social, emotional, and cognitive aspects of teaching and learning. By including administrative, pedagogical, and essentials of leadership, all priorities are supported.

⚙️ What Works Best: Understanding the Influence of Your Program

Understanding the greater influence of your program can inspire persistence in working toward goals. From birth to age five, a high-quality program provides social, language, and cognitive stimulation that have lasting positive influences on academic and social outcomes (Fuller, Gasko, and Anguiano 2012). Warm and responsive relationships, play-based learning, positive guidance, and appropriately challenging experiences are essential to prepare children for school (Masterson 2018). Early language exposure that is rich in both quantity and quality and takes place through talking, interacting, and reading also has a positive long-term impact (Camilli et al. 2010; Weldon 2014). Children's language skills from age one to two years predict their preliteracy skills at age five (Kuhl 2011). Their vocabulary level at the age of three predicts reading at third grade and future academic success (Zauche et al. 2016). Ensure that your program staff know the importance and influence of their work.

Aiming for Excellence and a Journey of Growth

Tabitha returns from a leadership conference feeling inspired. She posts a sign on her office door: "We teach children skills for life." In a staff discussion about using language prompts during play, Joshua remarks, "We have a long way to go to reach our goals." Tabitha responds, "How do we know we're making progress?" The usually responsive group is silent. Finally, Melissa answers, "I see progress when a child uses descriptive words during play." Sue adds, "I see progress when a parent thanks me for what a child is learning." Tabitha says, "We are working toward long-term goals and also celebrating the short-term accomplishments that we see. Let's take time each week to talk about the progress we're making."

When you play a board game, the goal is to move all of your pieces into a designated area, be the last one standing, or achieve the most points before—or with—everyone else. You experience an exhilarating sense of victory, thrill at making the right move, or pride in choosing an effective strategy.

Your professional life may not have such clear markers of success. How do you measure the daily significance of building relationships with teachers? How will you recognize the effects of excellent teaching when learning happens in incremental steps? How do you know that the resources you share make a difference to your staff? Given the unseen outcomes and gradual development of change over time, it is important to recognize and celebrate progress.

It is human nature to enjoy the successes of others and to cheer on the progress of teammates. A spirit of positive energy and expectation is often contagious. The following strategies will jump-start your journey:

- **Be an encourager.** Everyone appreciates a cheering section: "I am in your corner." "I'm thinking of you today as you try a new strategy. Let me know how it goes." "I noticed you stayed late to meet with the families. That will make a difference."

- **When you experience setbacks, get right back into the game.** Use challenges as opportunities to reorient your thinking patterns: "This happened today, but I'm going to approach this differently tomorrow."

- **Keep the focus on opportunities.** "You encountered a challenge, but you're making progress." "You weren't sure what to do this time, but now you have strategies to use next time."

- **Create short- and long-term goals.** While children's social development takes time, encourage teachers to use one new positive guidance strategy each week. Children's literacy skills develop over time, but in the short term, you can ask teachers to set a goal of reading two new books each week. Building relationships with families takes time. Encourage teachers to share a positive contribution children have made during daily pick-up time, so that families hear five affirmations about their children's developing competencies each week. Worthy goals begin with small steps.

- **Encourage the health and wellness of your team.** Support your team's efforts toward health and wellness, including organized schedules, consistent exercise, adequate sleep habits, and work-life balance. Be a positive role model for growth.

Influencing Leadership through Vision and Practice

Phyllis stops by Iris's office on her way home. "We're moving to Georgia after the holidays. I want you to know how much Kody and Kennedy have loved being in your program. These are memories we'll cherish for years to come. We found a great program for them to attend that is sponsored by my husband's new job."

Iris responds, "Thank you, Phyllis. Families like you make my job so rewarding. Your two beautiful children have had a great start in life. I know their teachers and friends will miss them."

The work you do is your legacy. To children who come through your doors, you imprint the power of language. You give love and security that becomes a blueprint for future relationships. You instill a sense of purpose to serve others and contribute productively. You inspire a love of learning. To families you serve, you reinforce and foster competence. You empower engagement and build on their investment in the lives of children. To your staff, you model professionalism. You demonstrate healthy leadership and model how to invest in the skills of others.

Your work has a profound impact on children, families, staff, as you provide a stable and economically sound anchor to your community. Your thriving business strengthens your community. Your involvement in professional organizations extends your influence outward into the greater world. Those who lead also have the benefit of growing in leadership skills and influence.

As a program administrator, it is likely that your work is your passion. As you explore each area of the Whole Leadership Framework, you will gain a new perspective on the importance of your work. You will see how your daily work is energized by your mission, your leadership, and your commitment. You will begin to link daily investment in the work of your program to long-term outcomes for staff, children, and families.

0—x Legacy of Leadership: Living Your Best Life

"After my children started school, I realized how important the first five years are to their development. I achieved my state director's credential and took on the role of program director. While talking to my mom, I apologized that I didn't stay in nursing. But I realized that my choice was exactly what I wanted to be doing. This is my best life—the profession I am called to serve. I have begun to read books, attend conferences, and embrace growth. This is the best journey ever."

Take-Away Strategies: Developing a Purpose Statement

To chart the course toward your vision, you must define the vision. It helps to think about the motivating purpose behind your work and to consider the personal and interpersonal context of your interactions with others. The following questions will help you develop a statement that can inspire and guide your daily work.

1. What inspired you to serve children and families? What drew you to this profession?
2. Leadership includes both an outward and inward focus. Why is it difficult to keep an outward and inward focus during a typical day? What purpose or personal mission statement will help you keep a balance?
3. Create a purpose or personal mission statement that will refocus your vision and empower your work on a daily basis.

Chapter 1 Study Guide: Exploring Influence

Influence through Inspiration and Motivation

Influence is defined as "the capacity or power of persons or things to be a compelling force on or produce effects on the actions, behavior, opinions, etc., of others" (*The American Heritage Idioms Dictionary* 2018). In your role as a leader, you are in a position to be influential in the work you do. Your knowledge of the Whole Leadership Framework and implementation of the practices within each component will increase your influence both internally and externally. This chapter encourages self-discovery related to your role as an influencer.

Below, list at least five examples of ways you inspire and motivate staff. Next to each, list its relationship to influence.

Inspirations and Motivations	Relationship to Influence
I post inspirational quotes in the staff lounge.	Staff are more positive. Staff know I care.

Reflect on the list above. Do inspiring and motivating staff come easily to you, or do you struggle to provide encouragement? How does inspiring and motivating staff relate to influence?

Consider how the conversations you have with staff affect their feelings and actions. Provide an example of the way a conversation you had influenced the feelings and/or actions of a colleague.

_____

_____

_____

Reflect and describe how to use your influence in positive ways that help staff to grow.

_____

_____

_____

Influence and Power

Influence is often associated with power. Take a moment to assess how you feel about power by selecting the statement that best applies to you:

☐ I believe that if I give staff more responsibility and opportunities to take on leadership roles, such as facilitating meetings, representing the center on committees, making decisions, and supervising others, I will then lose some of my power and influence.

☐ I believe there are limited opportunities for power and influence within my organization; therefore, if I entrust others with these opportunities, I limit my opportunities for power.

☐ I believe that if I share my leadership responsibilities with staff, they become empowered. Then I am able to focus on different and new opportunities, and our organization benefits.

☐ I believe it is important for all staff to take on leadership responsibilities as we support one another, and staff should routinely take turns leading tasks.

Now, reflect on the statement you chose. Do you behave as if power is limited, or do you behave as if power is infinite? How do your beliefs about power influence the staff in your center? How do they influence operations? How do they influence staff involvement? How do they influence staff attitudes? Do you want to change anything regarding your beliefs about power?

_____

_____

_____

_____

_____

_____

_____

Do You Lead Like a Goose?

There is a popular story about influence related to an unlikely source: a flock of geese. You many have noticed that when geese fly, they are arranged in a V formation. This is not purely coincidental. Geese fly in this way because it conserves energy. By flying in a V, there is a reduction of wind resistance for the geese who are following. Thus, the geese are able to fly faster and farther than if they were flying solo. In addition, the V formation makes it easier to keep track of one another and communicate. You may have noticed that fighter pilots also use this strategy. When geese fly this way, it seems there is a clear leader of the pack; however, they take turns in this role. The goose in the lead is exerting the most energy and will eventually fall back in the formation and allow another goose to take on the lead position. During flight, the geese also honk repeatedly, which has been reported to be encouraging to the other geese. When a goose gets injured and needs to leave the formation, one or two other geese follow along. They stay together until the injured goose dies or is well enough to join another flock.

The habits of geese represent a mindset about power that is inclusive. The geese share power and leadership. How does this story relate to the leadership exercised in your program?

Level of Influence

Consider your level of influence in each of the whole leadership domains: leadership essentials, administrative, and pedagogical leadership. Would you like more influence or less influence in any of the domains? Explain why.

If you would like more or less influence in a domain(s) of whole leadership, what action steps can you take to change your level of influence?

What resources, such as time, people, books, journals, training, and so on, do you need to assist you in changing your level of influence?

Building a Foundation: Leadership Essentials

Lucy, the director of Cozy Corner Child Care, regularly updates the program handbook. During this process, she seeks feedback from staff: "What procedures do families easily understand and follow? Where should we make changes?"

Josefina, the toddler teacher, asks, "Isn't it obvious that things have to be the same for everyone?"

Lucy responds, "Just like teachers, families appreciate knowing what will happen and what they need to do."

Josefina agrees. "I guess our job is to be sure everything is predictable."

Lucy nods. "Predictable routines and expectations help families and children transition smoothly from home to the program."

Lucy includes her staff in conversations about the family handbook and expectations because she knows that asking them to give feedback also helps them understand its purpose. By exploring the topic together, they are more likely to feel comfortable communicating with families. Lucy wants to build consensus among her staff by inviting questions and strengthening their understanding. She knows involving them in decision making builds teamwork and positive regard.

In their article "Leadership Development for a Changing Early Childhood Landscape," Martha Muñoz and colleagues assert, "Leaders are not simply born. They possess a combination of skills that can be identified, understood, learned, and practiced." Leadership essentials are the foundational competencies necessary for all areas of your work. They include the skills and competencies you need to foster a healthy organizational climate. Whether you think of yourself as an administrative leader or as more of a pedagogical leader, these competencies will make you more effective.

Leadership essentials are often expressed in personal styles of leadership and dispositions, such as self-efficacy, empathy, creativity, authenticity, humility, transparency, adaptability, and ongoing learning. When it comes to personal attributes, some may come naturally and others might not. Although some may be easier for you to develop, all can be strengthened through reflective practice.

It is often easier to focus on the immediate and visible tasks, such as the physical environment, guiding behavior, managing meals, overseeing activities, keeping up with business records, and communicating with families. It requires intentional reflection to think about the way approaches, dispositions, and interpersonal skills affect the effectiveness of daily tasks and activities.

Leadership essentials promote program norms; activate processes for growth; ensure trust and transparency; and ensure healthy dialogue, feedback, and collaboration. You are the one who can foster a positive emotional climate, encourage positivity and respect, inspire belonging and purpose, and cultivate a safe culture for growth. Leadership essentials will help you ensure strength-based communication and approaches.

By strengthening your leadership essentials, you will be able to identify and build on the capacities, resources, and strengths of your staff. You will be able to increase collaboration among your team. Growing in knowledge of the profession will help you develop new strengths and skills. Becoming transparent and adaptable and embracing life-long learning are behaviors and attitudes that can be strengthened and will return great joy and satisfaction in your work.

The following chart presents the elements of leadership essentials, including the personal attributes, tools, and impact on the health and vitality of your organization. The following sections explore the personal attributes in detail. Chapter 3 will present the tools for leadership essentials and how these facilitate excellence and effectiveness in your work.

Elements of Leadership Essentials

Personal Attributes	Tools for Leadership Essentials	Impact on Organizational Health and Vitality
Self-efficacy	Communication and team-building skills	Influences all areas of leadership vision and practice
Empathy	Awareness of self and others	Cultivates an emotionally healthy organization
Creativity	Cultural competence	Ensures a productive work environment
Authenticity	Ethical conduct and morality	Fosters collaboration, efficacy, and creativity
Transparency	Intentionality	Maximizes human capacity
Humility	Ability to motivate people	Encourages open, honest communication
Adaptability	Knowledge of the profession	
Learning	Management skills	

Understanding the Power of Self-Efficacy Beliefs

Elisabeth, the director at Little Learners, concludes a meeting with Tanya, the pre-K teacher, and Beth, the parent of Max. She assures both of them, "I am confident that we can work on this together. Tanya can adjust the morning schedule as we help Max feel secure in the transition from home. Many children need this extra support. We will encourage Max here, and you can work with him at home. Planning a special morning ritual has worked well for others."

Leadership essentials include the important quality of self-efficacy. This program director has used words such as *together* and *confident* on purpose. She explains that other families have struggled with difficult transitions in the morning. The program staff have been successful in helping other children adjust during arrival. She instills the idea that competence and success are something people achieve by working together. Albert Bandura, author of *Self-Efficacy: The Exercise of Control*, defines this quality as belief in one's personal capability and resources to meet the demands of tasks and to reach defined goals.

Two directors may face the same challenge, yet only one may embrace it with confidence. How does self-efficacy affect one's approach? When you were a child, if someone communicated that you were smart but you then struggled or failed, you may come to believe that success and failure are due to circumstances outside your control. But if someone gave you feedback about the strategies you used and encouraged your persistence and effort, you are more likely to have developed the belief that you have control over your successes. This is the heart of self-efficacy—the belief that if you work hard and use effective strategies, you can develop competence that leads to success.

Self-efficacy strongly influences the way people think they will handle events and situations (Kelleher 2016). In this way, self-efficacy influences thought patterns—whether you talk to yourself in self-defeating or self-supporting ways when you face challenges (Bandura 1986). Self-efficacy also affects resilience—whether you rebound quickly when faced with difficulty and setbacks or struggle to move forward (Masterson and Kersey 2013). A person with high self-efficacy is motivated, persistent, goal directed, and able to think clearly under pressure (McCormick et al. 2002).

Self-efficacy is strengthened when others encourage you. It also increases when you observe others you value and see them meet their goals. Your physical and mental well-being affect your perceptions too. Self-efficacy beliefs influence the way you evaluate the difficulty of challenges and how well you will be able to manage tasks over time. Leaders with high self-efficacy expect positive growth and hold high expectations for themselves and others.

You can apply your understanding of self-efficacy by encouraging staff when you see positive effort. You can notice and comment about strategies that worked well. Talking frequently with staff about their strengths, such as flexibility, positivity, and inventiveness, puts the focus on qualities that increase a sense of ownership. Offering resources of the program, such as your willingness to meet and talk about strategies and the opportunity to order books or training materials, can increase the idea that success is the result of planned steps. Brainstorming sessions allow staff to generate solutions to their own challenges and strengthen their sense of self-efficacy.

Importantly, you can be a strong role model as you share strategies you use to identify, work through, and bring solutions to problems you encounter. This shift in mindset helps staff view problems as opportunities for growth and reorients the focus from "stuck" to "strategic." Promoting the self-efficacy of staff supports a distributed-leadership approach. Remember that when you delegate some of your leadership functions to capable staff, you free up the time to fulfill the functions that only you can do. The following practical steps will help you energize your program's approach to learning and investment in positive solutions.

- **Define and post program goals.** "We prepare children for life." "Together Each Achieves More (TEAM)." "Families are teaching partners." "We empower lifelong learners." A shared motto communicates personal and shared capacity to reach goals.

- **Activate a kudos tradition.** Use a bulletin board, open meetings with cheers, and use a section of a newsletter to feature achievements. Your success depends on the full participation, strengths, and skills of your team. Notice and highlight positive contributions. Celebrate small victories.

- **Instill the practice of "plus one."** When you meet with staff—and when they meet together—ask them to describe effective strategies that solved problems or challenges. "I saw a helpful strategy you used with families." "That was a successful strategy to bring children in from outdoor play." Take notes and create concise handouts for staff that feature their own great strategies for positive guidance, language and literacy, science approaches, and verbal support strategies for play.

- **Provide multiple opportunities for collaboration.** Collaborative efforts help staff learn from and with each other and foster a sense of trust and comradery. Instill the idea that working together saves time and inspires brilliant solutions.

⚙️ What Works Best: Leader Self-Efficacy

Self-efficacy and its importance and contribution to leadership should be a priority for training and reflection (McCormick et al. 2002). Leaders' self-efficacy has a strong influence on the efficacy of the organization, including holding high expectations and creating a positive mindset of growth. The following are benefits to your program when you model self-efficacy:

- Collective self-efficacy in early childhood programs as a whole is one of the most important variables in teacher performance and effectiveness (Çalik et al. 2012). Model and encourage this mindset.

- Feeling competent, having strong relationships with others, and self-efficacy contribute to intrinsic motivation of all program staff (Ryan and Deci 2013). Establish and foster these dispositions through program practices.

- Shared staff efficacy has a positive effect on program outcomes, because staff work together to set high expectations, share achievable goals, and demonstrate commitment to children and families (Donohoo 2018).

- Self-efficacy helps staff manage stress in the work environment (Jeon et al. 2018).

- A person with high self-efficacy is motivated, persistent, goal directed, and able to think clearly under pressure (Bandura 1993). When leaders foster these norms, program work is more effective.

Fostering Empathy to Develop Social Capital

Teachers Jessica and Gemma struggle to push large cardboard cartons full of gloves, hats, and scarves across the hall to the gross-motor room, where they plan to sort the contents. The director, Cecilia, sees them trying to fit the largest carton through the doorway. She says, "Let's ask Keandra and Tori to help. They just finished a planning meeting." Cecilia goes down the hall and asks for assistance: "Jessica and Gemma have some sorting to do. They need six more cartons to be moved across the hall. Can you help for a few minutes?"

The teachers are quick to respond. "No problem! Let's get the sorting finished now, so we can distribute the gloves, hats, and scarves tomorrow."

As a program leader, Cecilia knows it is her responsibility to foster a culture of caring. Staff and families have collected gloves, scarves, and hats for children in their community. Modeling values of respect, service, and action has been an important mission of the program. Cecilia believes that children are more likely to take on these values when they see others engaged in caring. By involving staff, families, and children in experiences that promote empathy, she fosters social capital—the positive relationship connections among people who contribute to the program and its mission.

As part of Cecilia's program, philosophy, and approach, she emphasizes and discusses empathy during staff meetings. Empathy is posted as a goal in each classroom. A commitment to positive guidance ensures that all children receive fair and equitable support and are treated with empathy and respect. Teachers read books with characters who are empathetic in words and actions. Cecilia can see the effect a focus on empathy has made by the way her staff respond with cooperation and caring toward each other.

Empathy is a leadership essential that affects all interactions in a program. Empathy is more than a feeling or a recognition of the feelings and experiences of others. *Empathy* is the "ability to understand the feelings transmitted through verbal and nonverbal messages, to provide emotional support to people when needed, and to understand the links between others' emotions and behavior" (Polychroniou 2009). Activation of empathy as an organizational norm requires recognizing the importance of relationships as the foundation of program health and vitality.

Empathy requires the ability to understand others' perspectives and assume positive intentionality about their words and actions. This means that staff assume a "no fault" respect for the feelings and experiences of others (Tschannen-Moran and Tschannen-Moran 2014). It also requires awareness of the impact of one's words and actions on others. "How would I feel if someone brought something to my attention in that tone and style?" "Was this the right time, place, and situation to hold this conversation?" Healthy interactions stem from a balance of self and other awareness that leads to insight.

Program leaders are empathy gatekeepers of the organizational climate of the program. You stay tuned in to the "state of the program" by noticing nonverbal clues and using situational awareness to assess the dynamics of interactions. This information is critical, so that you know when to offer mediation or support. You can learn to address staff dynamics in proactive ways so as to foster needed empathy (Donohoo et al. 2018).

⚙️ What Works Best: Empathy Characterized by Action

Empathy enables program leaders to "develop an inclusive place where the highest aspirations of democracy are consistently at work, where community functions as it should, and where the best of human behavior is evident every day. It asks us to invest both our cognitive and affective energies toward those ends" (Tomlinson and Murphy 2018).

In this way, empathy is a cause for action. It is the ability to understand another person and the urge **to act** to increase another's welfare (Eklund et al. 2009). Empathy includes the action of reaching out to help (Marshall and Marshall 2011). Empathy in action is compassion (Pavlovich and Krahnke 2011). It means asking, "If I were in the same circumstance, what would I want or need?" It also means checking in with your staff to ask what they need. You may respond with a phone call, send a card, offer encouragement through physical assistance, or simply notice a tense situation and give verbal support. Empathy puts people first.

Empathy is a leadership essential that fosters culturally responsive practice. It requires reflection about subtle biases and examination of messages and practices to ensure inclusiveness for all who participate in your program. Key questions include, "What is the effect of this program policy or expectation on staff or on families? Do all have the opportunity for full participation and success?" Empathy creates common ground with others whose experiences are different from your own.

Empathy means matching staff potential and needs with opportunities to grow. You provide appropriate support when needed, because you are aware of contributing factors. Key questions include, "What do you need to be successful? What kind of verbal or physical support can I give to be helpful? What other resources will strengthen your work?" Empathy means appreciating people's strengths and giving them opportunities to shine. Empathy allows program staff to embrace common goals that are mutually beneficial as they honor the strengths and values of others.

Applying Creative Thinking to Your Daily Work

Bobbie, the director of Creative Learners Early Childhood Program, knows that the finances are tight—she needs to look for creative solutions. Three hours have slipped by while she tries to determine what budget line can be adjusted. She picks up the phone and calls a trusted colleague she knows from the community's director network, which meets monthly. "Mercy Ann, I'm stuck looking at the budget and all I can see are barriers. Would you have time for coffee? I would love for you to take a look and see if you can find what I am missing."

Mercy Ann responds, "I've been in that situation myself. Let's look for a creative solution together on Saturday."

You may think of creativity as something observable: creative websites, marketing materials, flyers, handouts, or wall displays. While creativity can be reflected in artistic endeavors, it is essential for leadership. Creativity is a mindset that invites people to explore problems and challenges from new perspectives. Instead of looking at an issue from a single angle, it invites exploration of new ideas and collaborative solutions that create a win-win outcome for all.

Some people feel they are naturally creative, but creativity can be cultivated and practiced. Creativity calls on people to think in new ways and apply innovative ideas to complex situations. Creativity encourages staff to share bright ideas. Creativity connects the dots from daily work to program goals. Everyone has unique, creative ideas and contributions that can foster insight and overcome challenges. Creativity moves people from a "right or wrong" mindset to one of flexibility and engagement. Instead of feeling stuck when encountering challenges, creativity removes limits and helps people become more effective.

In 2011, Mark Batey published a post in *Psychology Today* that suggests creativity is the most important skill for leadership. He notes that creativity is necessary on a daily basis for problem solving, and that fiscal profitability depends on creative use of human and financial resources. Importantly, with quickly changing professional requirements and standards of accountability, early adaptation is necessary for an organization to thrive. Leaders need to build a culture of creativity throughout programs to promote innovative thinking.

⚙️ What Works Best: Creativity Is a 21st-Century Skill

The Partnership for 21st Century Learning gathered experts and leaders in business and education to define the skills students would need for success in school, career, and the marketplace. These skills include creativity and innovation, critical thinking and problem solving, and communication and collaboration. These are competencies critical to the development of staff as well as children. Additional life and career skills include flexibility and adaptability, initiative and self-direction, social and cross-cultural skills, productivity and accountability, and leadership and responsibility. Program leaders have an opportunity to infuse and support creative thinking as a norm in the program and to foster creativity among staff (Stoll and Temperley 2009). For more information on the role of creativity in 21st century learning, see: http://www.p21.org/our-work/p21-framework

---

As a program leader, you have the opportunity to promote creativity and adaptive thinking. You can begin to think "outside of the box" as you plan and address issues. You can jumpstart habits of creativity in the following ways:

- **Brainstorm as part of daily personal practice.** When facing a problem, imagine multiple solutions. Many ideas will not be workable, but typically, you may find that your first ideas will not be the most effective answers. Make a habit of asking yourself, "What other ways are there of solving this problem?" Generate at least three new solutions. There are always multiple ways to solve a challenge or problem.

- **Implement an idea box.** Invite staff to contribute ideas both large and small that can help your program become more effective. Use those ideas to motivate discussion during staff meetings, which in turn may spur additional ideas and approaches to current issues.

- **Introduce brainstorming scenarios at staff meetings.** Ask staff to contribute issues and questions for discussion. Provide time for staff to write ideas, and then facilitate group discussion to pursue consensus. Ask your staff to implement the strategies and return to the following meeting to share how well these worked.

- **Use team-building exercises that foster collaborative solutions to problems.** While solving riddles, building with spaghetti and marshmallows, or making a balloon chain from floor to ceiling, staff can practice talking, listening, and working together to reach a common goal.

- **Provide coverage so staff can observe other classrooms.** Time spent observing professional peers can be an invaluable tool for creative learning. Typical staff responses include, "It helped so much to see how you do that." "Wow, I learned so much from seeing someone else read." "I wish I had known that strategy before."

- **Invite staff to discuss the topic of creativity.** Ask how creativity and originality help them teach. What aspects of creativity benefit the program? How can teaching and serving families become a more creative endeavor? How can staff think in new ways about teaching approaches, strategies, and collaboration with families?

- **Encourage teachers to share creative passions with peers.** One may share math games. Another may demonstrate how to use costumes and props during dramatic group reading. Someone may share innovative art projects for young children. When staff have frequent opportunities to talk about the aspects of teaching they enjoy, it creates an atmosphere of energy and investment in high-quality teaching practices and collaboration.

- **Invite families to participate in planning for activities and involvement.** Hold a focus group, send out surveys, and make phone calls. Creative input generates eager participation and shared responsibility for plans and events.

- **Extend creativity to external partnerships.** Invite local experts to share materials and provide training in organizational skills, teaching strategies, and reflective practice. Invite children's health professionals, library representatives, and local school personnel to meet at your program for coffee to discuss innovative ways to coordinate support for children and families.

Fostering creativity is a skill that requires openness to new ideas and perspectives. While active listening and planning require time and energy up front, the result will be staff who value participation. Creative conversation requires respect for ideas that may evolve over time. It can help to communicate, "Let's put this issue on the table and talk about it for a few weeks before we make a decision," or, "Let's meet once a month for six months." Extending the time frame for sharing ideas and processing challenges can yield fruitful solutions and can maximize buy-in from all participants.

Ensuring Authentic and Transparent Interactions with Others

At the morning tea, Amberlyn asks families to introduce their children's favorite kind of play and to share a dream for the future. Families respond, "I hope Arnab will be good in school and go on to college." "I want Adele to be strong and confident." "I wish for Jinani to be kind." Amberlyn replies, "Our staff share your goals and dreams for your child. They understand that you are your children's first teachers. You are an important partner in helping your child achieve."

Amberlyn's program has five new families from diverse cultural and linguistic backgrounds. She wants to put program goals into action and create an environment that feels welcoming. She and her staff meet to decide how bring this philosophy come to life. They decide to welcome the new families with a morning tea.

On the morning of the event, staff bring baked goods and decorate the meeting room. A translator is present for a family new to the United States. Handouts are available in home languages. Community resources and upcoming events are shared with the group. Each new family is joined by a mentor family—someone to check in with on a regular basis and to answer questions. Amberlyn invites them to a personal follow-up meeting. Rather than settle for superficial greetings, Amberlyn and her staff seek to build authentic relationships with families.

Authenticity is a leadership essential. Authentic leaders use their values as a guide for decisions and interactions with others and build relationships that inspire trust and commitment. These values are evident as the leader plans and carries out activities with staff. Authentic leaders are driven by their core values. They put their values into action and share them with others.

⚙ What Works Best: Benefiting from Authenticity

Authentic leadership is "a pattern of leader behavior that draws upon and promotes both positive psychological capacities and a positive ethical climate, to foster greater self-awareness, an internalized moral perspective, balanced processing of information, and relational transparency on the part of leaders" (Walumbwa et al. 2008). Authentic leadership raises the credibility of the leader and promotes effective relationships, staff engagement, team functioning, and productivity (Hannah et al. 2011). Authentic leaders put their ethical and moral commitments and ideals into practice no matter what pressures, challenges, or unique situations are present (Duignan 2014).

Authenticity is related to transparency, as values-driven leaders are more likely to be open about their thought processes, options, and choices. Transparency means being unguarded about the purpose of decisions and actions (Frederick et al. 2016). Transparent communication is "truthful, substantial, and complete" and includes reasons for actions and decisions (Jiang and Men 2017). Transparency is needed about staff roles and responsibilities, budget needs, short- and long-term planning, child assessments, staff evaluation processes, and opportunities for staff development. Transparency is communication that emphasizes shared knowledge.

⚿ Legacy of Leadership: Balancing Personal and Professional Responsibilities

"For the past year and a half, I struggled to balance my personal and professional life. I guess I was waiting for someone else to make a difference or to tell me what to do differently. I was doing the same things but expecting my day to go differently. I finally realized, 'There is no one going to change your life but YOU.' I blocked out a two-hour period each week for reflection and planning. I listed my strengths and wrote down my areas of challenge. I identified stress, physical wellness, and mental balance as the most challenging. I made changes to my schedule. I delegated tasks that were too much for me. I let others know my priorities and needs. Taking responsibility for my own experience has made all the difference."

Embracing Humility: It's Not about Me

> Vera is the educational coordinator of a Head Start program. She wanted to bring a math strategies workbook to the staff meeting, but she has forgotten to retrieve it from a colleague. "I'm sorry! I really want to support math talk, but it slipped my mind. I will be sure to bring it tomorrow. Let's brainstorm ideas and make a list. Jordan, will you lead the discussion?"
>
> Jordan says, "I have two great strategies to start. I used them yesterday with the morning preschool class, and it went well."

It is evident that Vera cares about the staff. She looks for ways to use their skills and build their competence. She asks for their input so that goals are met through staff-generated ideas and energy. Importantly, she wants them to be excited about the mission of the program, rather than have all the ideas and requests come from her. By putting staff in charge, she communicates that collaboration is an important trait for success. She also takes responsibility for her mistakes, knowing that she is modeling the message that growth, rather than perfection, is the goal.

⚙️ What Works Best: Humility Is a Strength in Leadership

Humility involves accurate self-appraisal of one's strengths and weaknesses and the ability to appreciate the strengths and contributions of others (Owens 2009). A humble person is teachable, willing to learn from the ideas and input of others (Oyer 2015). Humility serves as an important balance to self-confidence, as it helps leaders take responsibility for mistakes and readily accept feedback from others. A humble person admits mistakes and moves on quickly, taking responsibility to make things right.

For those who serve children and families, "humility is not a weakness, but a sign of acceptance and fearlessness by which leaders inspire others to be more of themselves" (Bruno et al. 2015).

Humility includes essential dimensions of leadership, such as serving the mission of the organization, commitment to learning, recognizing personal limitations, empowering others, accountability for actions, facilitating collaboration, seeing the big picture, serving others, and upholding ethical ideals (Caldwell et al. 2017). "Humility is not thinking less of yourself; it's thinking of yourself less" (Warren 2002). Thinking of others brings wisdom and insight to leadership.

Early childhood education is, at the heart, a service to and for people. A primary goal of program leadership is to support the professional growth and skills of staff so that they are equipped to be successful in their work. As your program grows, you will need to lead by influence and expand the talent and capability of your staff (Dunkley 2017).

A positive work climate is critical, as teachers who experience social and organizational support are more likely to feel greater well-being and engage in a higher quality of teaching (Jeon et al. 2018). A positive relationship with the program leader actually predicts less staff turnover (Wells 2015). Care should be taken to foster a culture of support and collaboration so that teachers love their jobs (Denham et al. 2017). For these reasons, accurate appraisal about the needs of staff and a commitment to empower their strengths is crucial.

Several strategies can strengthen a mindset of humility. These approaches focus on leader growth and fostering open communication and support for staff. Engaging staff in direct conversations about humility can encourage growth and impact program culture and morale.

- **Embrace personal humility.** Don't expect yourself to be perfect or assume that you will not make mistakes. This false belief will result in disappointment or upset when you can't deliver. Instead, embrace humility as freeing you from perfectionism and allowing you to participate in ongoing growth.

- **Place a high priority on wellness.** Don't hold yourself to unrealistic standards related to physical energy, rest, or nutrition needs, so that you become unbalanced in your approach to work. Instead, aim for wellness, so that you have the energy to think about others.

- **Make a list of strengths and limitations.** Ask a professional colleague, "Do you see these traits in my work? What else do you see that can give me insight into my work?" Plan to use your strengths and develop your weaknesses. How can you use your strengths in new ways? How can you grow professionally?

- **Turn struggles into opportunities for growth.** When you struggle with new technology systems, encounter conflict, or want to boost your own competence in a specific area, work together with a coach or peer. Being responsive to struggles can turn them into opportunities for positive growth.

- **Model humility in practical ways.** You don't have to be right. You don't need credit. You don't need to know it all. The greatest strength is often shown through gentleness. Take time to focus your thoughts and think of the outcome you want to create. What can you say—or not say—that will bring about a positive conclusion or resolution to an issue? How can you use a teachable moment to strengthen the skills, confidence, and commitment of others?

- **Make sharing progress in a safe setting a program norm.** Provide time for staff to share what they have learned, noticed, or implemented differently. When conversations about growth are frequent and supported, staff feel safe sharing their experiences. Open communication fosters a growth mindset and establishes humility as a program norm.

In the middle of daily stresses and unexpected interruptions, purposeful humility—pausing to recognize that you don't have all the answers—allows you to keep things from "being about you" and instead shift your focus on working together with others (Guilmartin 2010). Patience and humility communicate the belief that all members of a program have valued talents, skills, and contributions (Wasonga 2010). The idea that you are in this together is powerful and fosters a sense of collective organizational pride. The result is a spirit of humility and mutual appreciation.

Fostering Adaptability

Just as Marilyn's teachers had adapted to the previous assessment tool, the state quality rating and improvement system (QRIS) shifted to new requirements. "How am I supposed to shift my thinking?" Chloe leans on her hands and sighs. "Our teaching team just got proficient using the current system. How will we learn this in time for the evaluation?"

Marilyn responds sympathetically. "I can understand how this feels, but we'll learn together. I've invited a coach to come. She'll spend time with each of you and make sure you have what you need. You're not responsible to make the shift alone. We will learn together."

While it is natural to resist change, early childhood leadership is a profession that requires—and at times demands—change. Research introduces new information about teaching. You may learn more effective strategies for administering your program. Licensing requirements are revised often. Documents and records need to be updated. Food-reimbursement guidelines are modified frequently. Requirements for staff professional development are increased. The assessment data you are asked to collect requires a new online technology system. You will be confronted almost daily with change.

To embrace growth, it helps to recognize that human beings are designed for consistency. You may like things to stay the same. People and experiences, including cultural settings and situations, that are familiar feel pleasurable (Wexler 2008). Doing something the same way over time may cause you to feel comfortable and safe. Changes to job requirements challenge your sense of equilibrium and can cause psychological discomfort. It is natural to revert to and prefer what you already know. For these reasons, flexibility is a trait that requires commitment and practice. You may need to reorient your thinking and approach to view change in a positive light.

Carol Dweck discusses growth in her ground-breaking book *Mindset: The New Psychology of Success*. She introduces the importance of developing a growth mindset. Embracing growth fuels a passion for learning. However, to embrace growth, you have to be willing to live outside of your comfort zone, especially during times of change.

The ability to embrace change as a positive opportunity depends on your beliefs about the availability of resources (your own and your organization's) to meet the demands. Flexibility means you make quick adjustments, let go of minor issues, and move on. You use ongoing reflection and self-awareness and are quick to respond to others and the needs of a situation.

Adaptability means fine-tuning today what did not go so well yesterday. It means getting to sleep earlier when fatigue becomes a regular companion. It means tending to inflexible reactions until you begin to be flexible again. When productivity turns into stress, pay attention to the processes of balance. *Balance* means maintaining perspective about your priorities and goals. Balance is dependent on the leadership essential of flexibility and adaptability to change.

From a leadership perspective, change is about growing with others, not keeping up with or outpacing them. You grow most with the shared wisdom and support of colleagues. Big accomplishments are the result of small steps taken in collaboration with others. One conversation after another, you work together toward solutions. One brainstorming session after another, you gain insights and new ways of thinking. You embrace change bit by bit, day after day—with the support of others.

O━┱ Legacy of Leadership: Using Change as an Opportunity to Grow

"It seems like I just figure out how to do something when I face changes in the state policy environment or national quality expectations. Why do I need to learn new ways? My self-protection kicks in, and I feel like responding, 'Are you kidding? Don't you respect the way my programs are currently serving children and families?' I have had to work hard to shift my thinking and become more flexible. I try to look at changes in the external environment as opportunities to grow. I remind myself that I want my programs to be learning organizations in which children, families, and staff continuously learn, grow, and develop. Updating my leadership skills—walking the talk—is an ongoing part of this work."

Aiming for a Passionate Learning Mindset

Jada is the first to arrive at the local child care resource and referral training site. "I'm excited to hear the presentation. I'm going to take notes and see what I can do differently. I need to save myself some time."

Aletta sighs. "I need the help, too. I've been struggling with time management. Maybe tonight I can learn how to shift things around."

The presenter laughs, "I think I will learn as much from you as you will from me. Let's see what we can figure out together."

Aletta attends a networking group in her community. For several months, she has made phone calls and planned a presentation by a motivational speaker on steps for effective time management. The group stays late, enjoying the camaraderie and learning. They decide to meet again. Over time, they become a cohort group for professional learning. Together, they take online coursework, participate in webinars, and attend conferences.

Passionate learning is a leadership essential. Administrative success is supported by competencies in organizational leadership. Interpersonal communication, coaching, mentoring, stress management, problem solving, and personnel management can strengthen these skills. Program effectiveness can be strengthened through business and technical practices, legal knowledge, and budgeting skill. Leaders build on professional foundations, research in the field, and on best practice.

Pedagogical training requires a comprehensive set of knowledge, dispositions, and skills for teaching and family outreach. Continuous improvement efforts, such as a priority on positive guidance, social skills, and child development, can positively affect the quality of the setting, materials, curriculum, and interactions. As a pedagogical leader, you support your teachers in teaching goals and ensure that practices in the program are research based and data informed. Over time, you develop a wealth of knowledge and a wide range of skills to guide the direction of your program.

While daily demands of meetings, calls, and management tasks often take precedence, time invested in professional growth is essential. A passionate learning mindset is one of the most important drivers of quality and ongoing improvement in of all aspects of your program. While many leaders participate in coursework, conferences, and leadership academies, the most important kind of professional growth happens over time by participating in a cycle of reflective practice.

Leadership essentials grow in the context of reflective practice. *Reflective practice* means being intentional about observing, documenting, questioning, and evaluating—processes that are a natural part of learning. Reflective practice also is a mindset about learning from day-to-day experiences. It requires intention, honesty, and willingness to grow and happens in partnership with others as you invite them to grow with you.

Reflective learning builds connections between what has happened and areas for improvement and growth. It involves thinking critically about what works and why—and what can make you more effective. What are the dynamics at work? What are the hidden processes, assumptions, or barriers? What can you learn from this situation that can be applied to future interactions? Reflective practice requires an engaged mindset, a vision for growth, and intentionality. The following are strategies to jump-start reflective practice:

- **Invest in yourself.** Take time each day to foster your own growth. Find and schedule professional growth opportunities, including webinars and online learning, conferences, a program leadership training group, a director's roundtable, or monthly support and learning meetings. Take a class at your local community college or university. Participate in your state's QRIS. Invest in your profession to increase professionalism and advocacy for early childhood leadership. Organizations like the McCormick Center for Early Childhood Leadership can help you reach your program goals.

- **Use a working notebook.** After an event or interaction, record what worked well and what you want to do next time. How could you have prepared differently, interacted more sensitively, or modified what you did or said? What did you do well that you want to repeat?

- **Keep an opportunities journal.** This private writing space can help you dig more deeply to explore meaningful and productive pathways of growth and consider fruitful ways to promote change. Here, you can follow more complex pathways. Capture your insights, ideas, dreams, and possibilities. Evaluate the effect of your attitudes as well as your actions. Take time to consider readiness for change in your program. What are the barriers and opportunities?

- **Begin a dialogue group.** Because leadership requires mutual interdependence and influence, it requires reflective practice in the company of others. Your dialogue group can take many forms: coffee with a colleague on a regular basis, a community of practice with program directors, a lunch-and-learn meeting with your program staff, or an online book club to focus on professional growth. Growth requires trust, so set norms, including confidentiality. Your purpose is to share wisdom, to reflect, and to learn from each other.

⊞ Take-Away Strategies: Applying Leadership Essentials to Your Work

Early childhood programs are staffed by people from differing backgrounds and experiences. The interpersonal dynamics can raise challenges on a daily basis. To create positive outcomes, consider the areas of work that most affect your energy, focus, and priorities.

1. Describe the three most challenging aspects of program leadership. These are the areas that require time and energy and often create stress.

2. What important insights have you learned about relational dynamics at work?

3. What keeps you from being at your relational best?

4. What dynamics would you like to change in your work place?

5. What one attribute or trait would you like to change about yourself?

6. How can leadership essentials—self-efficacy, empathy, creativity, authenticity, humility, transparency, adaptability, and learning—influence the outcome of your challenges?

Chapter 2 Study Guide: Exploring Leadership Essentials

Learning Leadership

"Leaders are not simply born. They possess a combination of skills that can be identified, understood, learned, and practiced" (Muñoz et al. 2015).

How does this quote resonate with you? Do you believe it is true? If so, what leadership skills have you learned since becoming a leader in your current role? List some below.

_____

_____

_____

Take time to reflect on how you learned these skills. Did you learn them by attending training, through work with a mentor or coach, or as part of an orientation, or did you learn them through experience?

_____

_____

_____

Learning Leadership Essentials

Refer to your list of leadership skills that you have learned since becoming a leader in your current role. Check all those that relate to leadership essentials. Next, determine which leadership-essential attributes you feel you would benefit from learning more about.

☐ Self-efficacy   ☐ Transparency

☐ Empathy   ☐ Humility

☐ Creativity   ☐ Adaptability

☐ Authenticity   ☐ Learning

Benefiting from Leadership Essentials

Self-efficacy, or the belief in one's personal capability and resources to meet the demands of tasks and to reach defined goals (Bandura 1997), is a leadership essential. Having a sense of control over situations makes you more likely to persist and makes you more patient when staff need more practice to be successful with a task. These are just two benefits of having a leader who demonstrates self-efficacy. Take moment to jot down a few more:

_____

_____

_____

Similarly, having a leader who demonstrates empathy, creativity, authenticity, humility, transparency, adaptability, and learning is beneficial. Review each of these leadership essentials in this chapter. Reflect on the benefits of each, and write your thoughts below.

Leadership Essential	Benefits
Empathy	
Creativity	
Authenticity	
Humility	
Transparency	
Adaptability	
Learning	

Leadership Essentials in Practice

Consider how you demonstrate each leadership essential in your work. Provide examples below.

Leadership Essential	Demonstrated Examples
Self-efficacy	
Empathy	
Creativity	
Authenticity	
Humility	
Transparency	
Adaptability	
Learning	

What conclusions can you make about how you demonstrate leadership essentials in your work from doing this exercise? Is there a leadership essential you favor? Is there a leadership essential you would like to practice more?

What prevents you from demonstrating the leadership essentials more, and what resources or practices could be put in place to help you develop each leadership essential to its fullest potential?

_____

_____

_____

_____

Leadership Essential	Condition Preventing Demonstration of Leadership Essential
Self-efficacy	
Empathy	
Creativity	
Authenticity	
Transparency	
Humility	
Adaptability	
Learning	

What resources, such as time, people, books, journals, training, and so on, do you need to assist you in improving your leadership essentials?

_____

_____

_____

The Challenges of Leadership

Describe three organizational challenges that are a struggle.

_____

_____

_____

Do any of these challenges relate to a leadership essential (self-efficacy, empathy, creativity, authenticity, humility, transparency, adaptability, and/or learning)?

_____

_____

_____

Embracing Growth through Adaptability

List three changes on the horizon in your program.

_____

_____

_____

Most of us find it easy to list all of the reasons not to implement a proposed change. This exercise focuses on the leadership essential of adaptability. Select one of the changes you listed above, and list as many advantages as you can think of for implementing the change. You may want to consider the following.

- The impact of this change on the program, families, and staff in general, and on individuals.
- How the change relates to trends in the field, society, and technology.

_____

_____

_____

Use these advantages to drive the change.

Applying the Tools of Leadership Essentials

Tools for Leadership Essentials

- Awareness of self and others
- Knowledge of the profession
- Communication and team-building skills
- Cultural competence

- Ethical conduct and morality
- Intentionality
- Ability to motivate people
- Management skills

Activating Communication and Team Building

> Rachel starts the coffee pot, opens the blinds, and answers emails. At 7:00, she heads down the hall and pokes her head into the pre-K room. "Good morning, Irena and Jasmine. Make it a good day!" As she arrives at the front door, Rachel hugs children and greets their parents. "How are you feeling, Ms. Ruiz? I am glad to see you back." To Mateo, she adds, "You are getting so big!"
>
> Ms. Ruiz responds, "Mateo is already wearing his brother's coat."
>
> Rachel says good morning to other families. "Enjoy the day." "Glad to see you."

Rachel has a pressing list of phone calls and paperwork waiting for her. But she knows her visibility with families has a positive effect on the emotional climate of her program. Greeting teachers and families is an important extension of the philosophy and mission of the program.

Rachel's regular presence in the morning cultivates predictability and trust. She is committed to creating a healthy workplace environment for teachers and staff. Families feel reassured that their children are in competent and safe care. Rachel's daily interactions, smiles, and encouragement are an important part of the children's experience, as well. They feel comfortable, safe, secure, and welcomed. Rachel knows her example shapes the organizational climate.

Leadership is inherently relational. It is the transactional process of building your talent and ability, making the most of resources, and accomplishing positive steps toward shared goals. Team-building is much more than shared group experiences or organizing "get to know each other" games. Team-building means ensuring that the deepest motivational needs of the group are fully met. Some of the most important aspects of communication and team-building include the following:

- Encouraging dispositions of respect, positivity, and optimism
- Inspiring a sense of belonging and purpose
- Encouraging ownership of success
- Affirming as well as building on individual strengths
- Developing shared goals and reflective practice
- Challenging each member to pursue excellence
- Cultivating a safe culture for risk-taking in pursuing growth
- Embracing individual differences as contributing to group strengths

The tools of communication and team-building are self-sustaining because they increase a sense of investment and shared mission. They strengthen the effectiveness of pedagogical and administrative activities. Skills for communication and team building foster open dialog about norms and expectations and facilitate healthy problem solving. They enable you to inspire commitment and ensure each person feels valued, needed, and appreciated. The tools for leadership essentials will activate needed skills and help you lead your staff in the dynamic and satisfying process of achieving your program goals.

⚷ Legacy of Leadership: Inspiring Respect among Staff

"Our kitchen staff work hard and get very little recognition or positive feedback. In spite of meeting dietary restrictions for vegan, vegetarian, and gluten-free meals for children in the program, teachers often grumble about the quality and temperature of the food. I decided to ask the kitchen staff to demonstrate at the next parent meeting how to prepare healthy, inexpensive, and tasty meals for young children. At the parent meeting, the 'kitchen ladies' showed families how to include seasonal and fresh ingredients in recipes children would enjoy. Families were invited to take samples home afterward.

"Our program staff attended this demonstration and gained new respect for our cooks. Families responded to the kitchen staff as if they were rock stars, and the teachers took note. After the event, our awesome cooks were no longer the 'ladies in the kitchen.' They became 'culinary experts.'"

Communication happens every time people are together. The direction of a conversation depends on the ability of the speaker to articulate needs and ideas and the ability of the listener to hear and respond to what is said. Verbal and nonverbal communication influence all aspects of organizational business: agreeing on responsibilities, making use of resources, solving problems, and creating action steps. Communication affects perceptions, morale, and motivation.

It is important to hear what others are saying, to know how to deal with conflict, and to be able support staff through difficult times. You can develop these skills through individual work and through professional development. The following approaches will help you keep communication productive:

- **Build on another's insights.** Let others know that you depend on their expertise and insight to facilitate a successful program. When you see something working well, take time to listen and learn. "How did you solve that problem?" "What works to keep you organized?" "How did you get them to work together?" Ask others to give their perspective. "You know your job best. Explain what you think is happening." "What do you think you need to make this work better?"

- **Practice active listening.** Set aside other concerns and focus on others as they talk with you. Reflect back what others say, paraphrasing and checking for understanding to be sure you really hear what is said, rather than imposing your own meaning. While it takes practice, you will become more comfortable with silence. Resist interrupting, and give others time to think and process their thoughts. Your active-listening skills will encourage others' willingness to share openly with you.

- **Solve current problems.** When you give feedback, focus on the present situation. "Today, I noticed that the bathroom was messy. Let's work together to keep it tidy." "Today, I noticed that you were still preparing when the children arrived." Staff may respond, "Thanks. I think I can manage this." They may ask for help or say, "I am not sure how to do this." Focusing on the current situation invites cooperation. This strategy also makes it easier for you to address situations as they happen.

- **Choose words carefully.** Words are never neutral; they encourage or discourage. They influence the beliefs and actions of others. "You are capable." "You matter to others." "Your work is important." "You have my support." Strength-based communication uses words that recognize, build on, and affirm positive outcomes. "I am confident that you can do this. I want to support your strengths."

- **Clarify and review.** When you need to address an issue, make a brief list of objectives. Affirm your partner, and define the purpose of the conversation. "I want to be sure we both understand what will be happening at the upcoming event." Revisit expectations. Ask for input. Make action steps. Be sure you summarize. Restate the needs, review your agreement, and restate the action steps. Be sure to set a time to meet to revisit how things went.

- **Keep emails neutral.** What is communicated in writing lasts. If you need to discuss a complex topic, set the meeting by email, but talk in person. Emails should be brief and positive. Hold important conversations in person, where you can be sensitive to body language and responsive to individual needs.

- **Activate staff strengths.** Identifying the strengths and abilities of others is an important task of leadership essentials. Create space for team members to contribute their ideas and skills. Tap into creativity, organization ability, writing skills, and personal attributes of staff. Foster emerging leadership by encouraging staff to plan meetings, lead a team exercise, or guide a teaching and reflection exercise.

- **Affirm others.** Thank staff for work well done. Let families and staff know how much you value their contributions. Start a kudos board to recognize outstanding effort. Add a "thanks very much" corner to your newsletter or weekly email. Provide a "great job" box in the office, and ask staff to write appreciative notes about those who have gone above and beyond. A spirit of appreciation will begin to permeate your program.

- **Use self-affirmation.** Positive thinking is a habit that takes cultivation and care. Words are powerful and influence the outcome of your communication with others. "I am confident and creative." "I am making progress!" Affirm your strengths and look for opportunities to share them. Self-affirmation can energize and refocus a challenging day.

To build a strong team, establish clear norms and expectations. Setting expectations for meetings and professional conduct is more than simply making or posting rules. Expectations involve attitudes, professionalism, work ethics, teamwork, quality of work, roles in supervision, and approaches to leadership. Norms include procedures for addressing problems in an appropriate manner and setting, the requirement to handle difficult situations calmly, and the expectation that all staff will seek positive solutions to problems.

Teamwork includes interacting with others in positive ways, listening well, offering assistance, respecting others' time and energy, and treating others with courtesy and respect. When expectations are introduced at orientation, revisited during weekly staff meetings, and discussed during supervision meetings, they become guiding principles for all relationships in your program.

Some norms are likely to be in line with professional standards and your program's philosophy. Other standards, such as professionalism during meetings, expected behavior in the school setting, and staff-related tasks, can be generated with group involvement, such as brainstorming and voting. When staff members take part in defining norms and expectations, you will gain a deeper sense of their background and understanding. Revisit norms at each meeting, and ask for revisions when necessary. When norms and expectations are clear, they will unite and inspire your team to work together.

🖼 Take-Away Strategies: Working with Staff to Foster Insight

Answer the following questions on your own, and share them with your staff. You will gain insight about one another's strengths, skills, and needs. You can also meet one-on-one to review these questions, then set action steps for growth.

1. What do you need to experience so that you feel highly valued?
2. What do you need to experience to feel fully supported in your work?
3. What would help you do your job better?
4. How would you describe being empowered professionally?
5. What is the most important strength you bring to the program?
6. What is the most important goal you have achieved in your job?
7. What is one goal you want to pursue?
8. What one core value is most important to you?
9. What would you like to do differently?
10. If you could change one thing that would make a positive difference to your work success, what would it be?

Boosting Awareness of Self and Others

Iris is the director of an infant-toddler center. Before a scheduled staff meeting, Iris asks Kerry, the assistant director, to observe closely and give her feedback. "I've been frustrated about how we track food use. When I talk with staff about this problem today, I want to be sure that I don't come across as upset. I want to be sure everyone understands the expectations and agrees to track food consistently."

After the meeting, Kerry responds. "I thought you made your point in a straightforward way. I thought staff responded well, and I heard positive comments made after the meeting."

Iris thanks Kerry. "I value your feedback. I want to set clear expectations and communicate confidence in staff support."

Relationship building is at the heart of the leadership. It is the tool that fosters trust, opens communication, and encourages healthy collaboration. Iris wants to be sure that she uses the meeting to revisit expected norms and communicate expectations for success. Getting feedback from a trusted colleague allows her to be accountable and to evaluate her communication.

Interpersonal skills are not a discrete set of abilities that are learned once and maintained. Effectiveness in leadership requires ongoing evaluation of attitudes, dispositions, and ways of approaching interactions. Previous understandings may not be adequate to help you make sense of a new situation. You will need to practice the art of reflection and seek counsel from others to gain insight and perspective. Interpersonal skills must grow and adapt constantly to be effective.

Honest appraisal of yourself and sensitive awareness of others are critical parts of leadership essentials. Whether intuitive or practiced, all leaders must consciously commit to the internal process of self-evaluation. What is your influence on others? What outcome do you hope to achieve? This kind of self-assessment will positively affect all areas of pedagogical and administrative leadership.

It helps to become aware of the ways your background experiences influence your perceptions, attitudes, and reactions, so that you see yourself honestly and choose to see the best in others. By becoming purposeful and reflective, you can be sure that you use accurate appraisals of yourself and others. The following strategies will help you become more strategic in reflecting on your perceptions, skills, and actions:

- **Practice self-management.** Do you say yes before evaluating whether you have the time, energy, and resources to follow through? Accurate evaluation of your abilities and priorities is essential. When someone asks for your time, respond, "Thank you for asking me. Let me look carefully at my calendar, and I will let you know before the end of the day." Perhaps you decide the task is something you want to do. Saying yes but modifying your time capability can save you from stress. "I would love to help out, but next week works better than this week. Would that time shift work for you?" Keeping your time and energy in balance is a priority.

- **Practice self-reflection.** *Self-reflection* means revisiting and fine-tuning honest awareness of your choices, actions, and words and noticing how these decisions affect subsequent choices and the reactions of others. Consider the effects of your choices and behaviors on staff and families. Be mindful of your actions, words, facial expressions, tone of voice, and inflection.

How would you evaluate yourself if your interaction were videotaped? What do others hear in your tone of voice? Did you wait until others finished speaking before you provided a response? Did you smile and lean forward while a parent talked with you? Were you breathing naturally and feeling relaxed? Asking these questions can help you become more mindful of your effectiveness and influence in the way situations turn out.

- **Foster the practice of self-reflection among your staff.** State the value of self-reflection as a priority in your staff handbook. Help staff identify their strengths and areas for growth. Ask them to consider prior experiences that foster their current strengths. Finally, provide time during staff meetings to encourage reflective conversation. Encourage the use of journals to record what happened, how things turned out, and what could be done differently. What are staff learning or wondering about that they can share and discuss with others? Revisit these reflections during individual staff supervision.

- **Ask for outside insight.** After an event or meeting, ask a trusted colleague, "How do you think that went? What could I do better? How did I come across?" Tell your colleague you value having a friend who can offer constructive criticism and want his help to become more effective in your interactions with others. Respond to feedback by saying, "I appreciate your perspective. I want to grow in that area to become more sensitive, skilled, and effective." Asking for feedback will help you reflect on ways to grow and adapt.

- **Reflect on your perceptions of others.** Projection is an incredibly powerful dynamic. Do you perceive others as kind and optimistic or as angry and critical? Perhaps you have brought this point of view to the interaction. Projection can keep you from seeing others clearly. Do you decide what you think or what should happen before you finish listening fully to others' input? Gather all information and perspectives before giving feedback. Take a moment to evaluate your internal emotions. Unbiased openness invites trust. Others will more likely relax and return your openness and trust.

- **Handle interruptions as opportunities to influence.** Do you feel your work life is filled with a constant barrage of unexpected challenges, events, daily happenings, people, and circumstances that you did not anticipate? Do you begin the day with your "to do" list but find that at 5:00 p.m., you haven't begun to tackle what you thought were your priorities? At times it feels the people in front of you are in opposition to your intended purposes. Instead, ask yourself, "What can I say and do to build this person's strengths and empower her growth?" The people in your program are your priority! Be "other-focused" to build up, encourage, and strengthen people.

- **Manage your reactions.** Owning your response can make your perceptions work for you, help you keep your composure, and make good decisions: "When ___happens, I feel___."

- **Take constructive steps.** Make a habit of asking, "What other ways are there to solve this problem?" Don't give up. Remember that there are always different ways of solving a problem. Too often, we try the same solution expecting a different outcome. Brainstorm multiple ways to approach a situation. Persist until you have a successful result.

- **Reframe challenging experiences.** Reorient challenges with positive actions. "I didn't handle that very well today, and I know what to do next time." "I am tired today, and tonight I will go to bed early and will start fresh in the morning." "I missed the cues. Next time, I will tune in more carefully." Remove the *buts* from your thinking: "I should have done that, but I didn't have time." Instead, speak honestly about what happened, and add an action step that will create a positive outcome next time. "I made a mistake, and I am taking steps in the right direction."

- **Revisit your mission.** Revisit your vision statement and mission. Your aim as a program leader is to strengthen others as people and as professionals. Keeping an eye on your goals can help you keep decisions and issues in perspective.
- **Monitor personal wellness.** Personal well-being can affect your perceptions and responses to others. Interpersonal skill requires a solid internal anchor to keep you steady when challenges come your way. When you are rested, it is easier to evaluate objectively all that you see and hear.

⚙ What Works Best: Honest Self-Appraisal

Accurate self-assessment of strengths, weaknesses, values, and contributions to interactions significantly affects the accuracy with which leaders evaluate circumstances and whether they communicate in appropriate and effective ways. (Hinkle 2018). Leaders need to be aware of their emotions, strengths, limits, values, and motives to make accurate evaluations of situations and conflicts (Goleman et al. 2013). Self-awareness includes being able to recognize your feelings and how they affect you, to stay tuned in to your own body signals, and to evaluate your thoughts and intentions as well as your impact on others (Nevarez 2017).

Self-appraisal is especially critical to culturally responsive leadership (Khalifa et al. 2016). A deep level of understanding is necessary to have a complete comprehension of the context of your program, families, and community. Leaders need awareness of the effect of their roles and practices as well as informed and accurate understanding of the dynamics of the context (Aas 2017). Accurate self-assessment allows a leader to increase her effectiveness.

Items from a leadership-skills inventory (Bloom and Abel 2015) can help you evaluate strategies you use to foster collegiality. For example, do you listen attentively and respectfully? Do you ask thoughtful questions and seek to understand others' points of view and perspectives? When you give feedback, is it direct, respectful, and supportive? In the same way, are you able to receive feedback from others without becoming defensive? Do you diffuse conflict in a professional manner and help others find common ground? Presenting these questions as a staff reflection can encourage honest conversation and insight. Fostering a culture of reflection and self-appraisal is necessary component in healthy organizational growth.

🔑 Legacy of Leadership: Inviting Reflection

"The best advice I can give is to address problems as they occur. Don't wait and second-guess yourself. When you do bring something to a staff member's attention, don't elaborate, give details, or blame. Simply state what you observed: 'I notice the transition was difficult yesterday. What do you think about what happened?' Open-ended questions invite reflection, open sharing, and honesty. When you hear a response, don't offer suggestions. Instead ask, 'What do you think is a good solution?' Often what people need most includes support and a safe place to talk through ideas and action steps. When you address things immediately, it keeps the air clear, gives staff opportunity to explain their point of view, and invites problem solving."

Fostering Cultural Competence

On Tuesday morning, director Anika has an appointment scheduled to meet with Palani's mother to talk about the child's need for language support. When Anika opens the door, she is surprised to find that Palani's father, older sister Nishka, grandfather, grandmother, aunt, and mother are all present. Anika greets them. "Good morning. I am glad to see you! Will you please give me a few minutes to find a location to meet?" After a few moments, Anika returns. "Come right with me. We can meet in the conference room upstairs."

When families come to discuss a learning, language, or behavior concern, often only one family member is present. But for this Asian-Indian family, all are involved in the child's life and upbringing. Education holds a high value. To the family, attending meetings and being involved in Palani's school is a natural extension of their family life. But for this director, it was a surprise to see six people at the door when she expected only one. By responding warmly and making sure all family members were comfortable, Anika was able to learn much about Palani and his language needs. She established a strong foundation of trust with the family.

We live and work in a diverse world. Young children and families come from many cultures, but you may not know how to relate and communicate across those complex differences. Working on the skill set of cultural competence is critical. Cultural competence includes a commitment to learning about the families and communities you serve. It also requires flexibility to shift your preconceptions about ways that families are involved in their children's care. Cultural competence affects all aspects of leadership in your program.

Culturally responsive leadership begins with an evaluation and understanding of invisible barriers. Do all families feel comfortable entering your setting? Does the program experience for children and families provide a sense of belonging and the highest possibility of success? Is all information about success fully available to all family members? Are families included in decisions about children? In culturally competent organizations and schools, family strengths and resources are highly valued and understood as the source of a child's mindset, identity, and motivation.

You can also evaluate cultural responsiveness from children's perspectives. What do children experience when they enter the program or classroom? Do the materials, books, features, and photographs represent the lived experiences of the children? Has every teacher built on knowledge of children's experiences? Are high expectations placed on all children? Your program must communicate a sense of familiarity and welcome to all.

> ⚙️ ## What Works Best: Activating a Culturally and Linguistically Responsive Approach
>
> Cultural and linguistic competence in leadership places a priority on the beliefs, practices, and policies that offer fully inclusive experiences for children and families from ethnically and culturally diverse backgrounds (Johnson and Fuller 2015). Culturally responsive leadership includes the way staff evaluate and respond to the needs of children and families (Kalifa et al. 2016). This framework requires critical self-awareness and a deep level of commitment to inclusion, equity, and advocacy (Chen et al. 2009).
>
> Cultural and linguistic competence influences every area of your program effectiveness. *Culturally responsive family engagement* means that teaching staff embrace the multigenerational nature of families and include extended family members and nonrelatives who are involved in a child's life (Halgunseth et al. 2013). A full coparenting approach, with open communication and coordinated care, benefits children (Ruprecht et al. 2016). With a foundation of caring relationships, leaders must be inclusive in decision making. They must lead reflective conversations with teachers and staff about potential bias and stereotypes that can undermine trust, respect, and opportunity (Santamaría 2013).

Committing to Ethical and Moral Conduct

> Vera hangs back at center closing time. When the last family has left, Vera turns to the program director, Diana, and shares information about her home and boyfriend. She says that after a behavior issue, her son was asked to endure a prolonged form of punishment. "I don't know what to do," Vera blurts out. "I don't want it to happen again, but since it happened, Misha has been acting worse, and I am afraid. I haven't told anyone else." Diana listens attentively and says it is important for the child and Vera's safety to get help. Vera agrees to return in the morning to meet with Diana again.

As a program director, you are a mandated reporter. Diana's program is located in a large city. She develops close relationships with families and keeps extended hours to accommodate their schedules. As siblings come through the program, she finds herself struggling to keep professional and personal feelings separate and to make the right decisions when she feels parents are in survival mode. In this case, Diana is faced with an ethical challenge. She knows she needs to call child protective services and report the situation. The following months are difficult, but Diana's actions are in the best interest of the family.

There may be times when you are concerned about the possibility of abuse or neglect. You may witness or be told about situations by family members or by children. Child abuse and neglect can be physical, sexual, or emotional. Mistreatment may result in injury or may put a child at risk of injury. By law, you must report your concerns, even when you fear repercussions for the family. Diana reflected, "To manage my feelings, I tried to think about the child long term and what would be in the best interest of the family to break the cycle of abuse. Knowing that I followed through was an important step in my professional life."

As a program leader, it is important to lead with ethical conduct and morality. You need to "walk the talk" and lead by example to model ethical commitment and its application, so that your staff will be ethical in their behavior as well. Ethical behavior starts at the top. A leader who shows integrity serves as a positive example of why others should trust the work and people of your organization. You are a reflection of your program and lead by example when you show others that integrity is a core value of your organization.

As an early childhood professional, you commit yourself to the highest ethical standards, including bias-free practices in teaching and discipline; confidentiality in communication; and ethical practices related to business, personnel, and leadership approaches. A professional code of ethics provides standards or criteria by which you can weigh the many situations you encounter. This is the foundation of moral conduct in dynamic and complex organizations where people work together to serve children and families. Because you care for children who are too young and too vulnerable to protect themselves, you are held to an exemplary and uncompromising standard of ethical practice.

Personal values are similar to professional ethics and must be evaluated explicitly in light of stated professional mandates. A code of ethics presents the tenets of ethical practice with which you can examine and reflect on your decisions, interactions, priorities, practices, and impact on others. Feeney (2010) proposes that ethics are a professional responsibility carried out collectively and systematically by the membership of a profession.

The National Association for the Education of Young Children (NAEYC) *Code of Ethical Conduct* (2011) sets forth ideals, principles, and responsibilities of early childhood professionals. The first principle supersedes all others: "Above all, we shall not harm children. We shall not participate in practices that are emotionally damaging, physically harmful, disrespectful, degrading, dangerous, exploitative, or intimidating to children. This principle has precedence above all others in this code." This is the mandate for all leaders—to advocate for and ensure settings and relationships that are healthy, secure, and fully responsive to the needs of each child.

Early childhood leaders take responsibility to ensure that all children thrive and experience the highest quality of care and education. As part of your ethical responsibilities, you agree to promote respect for the dignity, worth, and uniqueness of families, including their strengths, values, expectations, language, and cultures. You agree to ensure bias-free practices regardless of family structure, race, national origin, religious and political beliefs, cultural practices, linguistic preferences, socio-economic status, educational level, disability, gender, or age. These commitments ensure that your program is safe, nurturing, and inclusive for all children and families.

Importantly, you demonstrate ethical responsibility toward your colleagues. You ensure a productive work environment that promotes respect, trust, confidentiality, and cooperation. You share needed resources for growth and continue to invest in staff development. You commit to ongoing communication and collaboration that lead to increasing growth and competence.

In an increasingly technological world, you will need to ensure privacy of information, including keeping conversations private and guarding the confidentiality and security of records, digital files, email, and identifying information belonging to family members. As someone who coordinates support services for early care and education, such as evaluation, assessment, and training, you have an additional layer of accountability for the ethical practices of others. Because your work is complex, you will need to review ethical standards and talk frequently and honestly about the areas of work that are challenging.

As a program leader, you have the privilege of entering spaces and evaluating human interactions that few have the honor to see. You will have the opportunity to support the growth of others, knowing and valuing their strengths and empowering their successes. You will support them in times of challenge and encourage them when they are stressed. You will be the beneficiary as you learn more about the privileges and opportunities of your influence as a leader.

Take-Away Strategies: Actualizing Ethical Conduct and Morality

- Exemplify the highest possible standards of virtue and practice (Cameron 2011).
- Ensure policies and conditions that are physically and emotionally safe and foster mutual respect, cooperation, collaboration, competence, well-being, confidentiality, and self-esteem (NAEYC 2011).
- Promote moral and ethical practice with and for children and families (NAEYC 2011).
- Use systematic evaluation of decisions, priorities, practices, and their impacts (Feeney 2010).
- Foster trust and authentic ethical conduct in all aspects of work (NAEYC 2006/2011).

Leading with Intentionality

A teacher is sick, and Sondra, the director of a community-based early childhood program, calls for backup. She looks up from the phone to see the copier service arriving and Mrs. Harvey, a guardian, waiting to say hello. After greeting her, Sondra tells Mrs. Harvey, "I want to connect again. Let's set a time to talk more." As she types a note into her phone calendar reminding herself to call the guardian, she sees a new hire waiting for orientation. With a smile, Sondra greets her and says, "Thanks for your patience." Sondra hugs two children who squeeze her knees and waves goodbye to Mr. George and Mikey. She points the repair service person in the direction of the copier and shakes the hand of her new administrative assistant.

On this typical day, Sondra stays patient and positive. These are her go-to habits. It may seem that these qualities come naturally, but Sondra is intentional about her choices. She didn't inherit a patient nature but learned the habits of caring for people from an aunt, who helped start this program eight years ago. Sondra often says that Aunt Reba always reminded her to keep her glasses clean, so she could see the important stuff clearly.

There is a popular saying about building habits. "Virtue is what happens when someone has made a thousand small choices requiring effort and concentration to do something that is good and right but doesn't come naturally. And then, on the thousand-and-first time, when it really matters, they find that they do what's required automatically" (Wright 2010).

You may wish that your many small choices would be easy ones. But the habits that matter the most often require attention and determination. Intentionality is a lens through which you view your relationship with the situations you encounter. Intentionality affects every area of your work and relates to how you balance your time across the leadership domains. To be successful, you have to examine these qualities in an intentional way.

Intentionality means being deliberate or purposeful. It means lining up your mental states (your thoughts, beliefs, desires, and actions) with specific goals. This requires a determination to act in a way that fits with your commitments and values. You may not be able to choose your circumstances, but you can choose how you will respond.

The words *intentional* and *tending* have the same Latin root word, *tendere*, meaning "to stretch." It may take purposeful stretching to embrace intentionality as a tool for leadership.

- Intend: to plan and aim
- Intention: sense of purpose
- Intent: absorbed and focused
- Intently: with concentration
- Intensify: strengthen
- Attention: concentration

Intentionality is a deliberate act of self-management. Self-management includes the ability to consciously have control over yourself and to choose meaningfully how you will respond to others. This is a discipline that takes practice and, at times, great determination. When you are intentional, you have the ability to shape the culture of your organization in a positive way. The following strategies will help you become more aware of the tool of intentionality and the ripple effect of its influence on other aspects of your program.

- **Post your goals**. Because you align your daily choices with specific goals, you can stay steady in the moment, keeping your line of sight focused. Will this decision take you closer to or further from your goal? Managing your energy and purpose is a critical part of your success.

- **Take ownership of your decisions.** Practice self-responsibility. Learn from your mistakes and celebrate successes. Mistakes are opportunities for growth.

- **Manage time.** Honor the time of others. Be intentional about setting aside time to meet with each of your staff. Be on time and end your meeting at an agreed-upon time. When you oversee your time in an expert manner, you can stay ahead of needed work and be proactive in keeping yourself on course.

- **Keep lists.** Each day, reprioritize your "to do" tasks. Separate them into "now" and "later." Divide them into "people" and "tasks." The benefit of a list is to reshape it at the beginning (or end) of each day and to use it as a road map to ensure you reach your destination.

- **Organize one space each day.** Tidy one quarter of your desk, one drawer, one bin, one mail pile, one window sill, any one small physical space daily. Start with a small area and focus only on that space. Giant strides are accomplished in very small increments.

- **Look ahead.** What can you do today that will make something easier tomorrow? What can you shift to tomorrow to open time to be available to people today? This mindset helps you be proactive rather than simply reactive to whatever comes your way.

The next time you face uncertainty, an unexpected change, a request that feels inconvenient, the need to learn a new skill, or a problem, how will you respond? Intention requires purposeful determination to align your thoughts, beliefs, desires, and actions with the goals you want to achieve. You can be energized through intentionality in action, as you focus on the important goals of your work. The essential tool of intentionality will support your energy and effectiveness.

⊠ Take-Away Strategies: Making Time for Project Management

Leadership empowers the success of the whole organization. You may share leadership roles and functions with others in the organization, but your organization as a whole requires vision, facilitation, guidance, direction, motivating energy, and project management. Project management affects all aspects of leadership. Personal, group, and organization-wide projects require careful attention and follow-through. *Intentionality* means making a clear decision to act or respond in a specific way.

- **Personal change:** Use a planning list. Make a phone call to get financial planning advice. Touch base with a mentor. Order an inspirational book or study guide.

- **Organizational change:** Use a project checklist or chart. Involve your staff. Describe where you are now and where you want to be. Create action steps and a time frame to achieve your goal. Identify needed resources and time. Revisit steps to make adjustments as needed.

- **External change:** Hold a parent event. Invite a pediatrician for a Q and A session. Attend a community director's event.

- **Discuss intentionality with staff.** What areas of self-management need attention? How can intentional planning increase effectiveness? Introduce these questions to staff and brainstorm solutions. Create a celebration board to highlight staff accomplishments.

- **Hold space and time for personal and organizational planning.** Spend ten minutes planning personal change, ten minutes planning organizational change, and ten minutes considering opportunities for external change. Reserve this planning time on your calendar.

Motivating People

> Marietta says, "Let's put the dollhouse on the low table for the younger children."
>
> Tara adds, "I have several boxes of books. Let's arrange them on the low shelf." Shaylene offers to decorate the bulletin board and hang curtains.
>
> Patrick says, "Two weeks ago, I would never have believed we could paint and refurbish the family center. But look what we have accomplished together. Our families are going to feel and experience the difference!"

Patrick became the director of this new center when his program consolidated with another. He realized the staff needed encouragement, so he asked them to decide on a program-improvement project they could work on together. Within two weeks, the beige walls were pale green, the trim was freshly painted white, and the change in spirit was palpable.

Daniel Pink, author of *Drive: The Surprising Truth about What Motivates Us* (2009), suggests that the secret to high performance and satisfaction at work is the deeply human need of people to direct their own lives, to learn and create, and to improve themselves and the world around them. Each person has an inborn desire to grow and to become better at what they do. They want to know that their contributions have value and that they matter.

Patrick's painting project with his new staff accomplished far more than brightened walls. During the mixing of paint and covering of floors with plastic, staff got to know each other. Over pizza and conversation, Patrick learned much more about the families and children of the center. The physical space came to represent the pride the staff felt in being asked what they wanted to change—and their shared leadership in getting it done.

Motivation results when people feel they have the support and resources they need to do their job well. Motivated engagement depends on a sense of autonomy—the feeling that staff members are trusted to make good decisions. Motivation also depends on an environment of encouragement and appreciation. You motivate teachers who work with children, support staff who make your program run smoothly, and families across your program.

0—🗝 Legacy of Leadership: Engaging Staff

"It was time to plan for our accreditation process, and I worried about getting my staff on board. I knew I needed to motivate them. I knew that buy-in was going to be important so that they owned the process. I asked what they knew about accreditation. What word associations, ideas, and feelings did they have about it? What prior experience did they have? I asked what they knew about the national organization. These conversations helped establish a common bond and laid the groundwork several months in advance.

"Once we moved past the preparation to the action stage, I asked my staff what skills they had that matched our action steps. 'What are you good at that can help us get this done?' They chose observation partners and organized fun games to learn the criteria. They decided to have portfolio pizza parties to work together collaboratively. We held weekly debriefing sessions to share feelings, concerns, and questions. When we achieved accreditation, the staff wanted to invite families to celebrate. We gave accreditation awards to each staff member for Best Supporting Laughter and Outstanding Organization in a Lead Role. The celebration of progress united our staff."

Positive change can be exhilarating and rewarding. Inviting people to participate in decisions, asking them for feedback, and letting them know their work matters can motivate them to invest their best efforts. Your example of investment and your positive engagement can influence the motivation of others. Motivation is an essential part of self-efficacy. Your example of clear vision, direction, and purpose invites others to participate and engage with you to make a positive difference for others.

Gaining Knowledge of Pedagogy and the Profession

> Marlene leans forward at the staff meeting to watch Ricca demonstrate a board game. James asks, "How did you get the children to play?"
>
> Ricca answers, "We tried the game first with a spinner and with the game drawn on a folder. The children played for only a few minutes. Then we tried a large counting cube to toss on the floor and recreated the game on a poster-sized board. Moving from table to floor made the difference."
>
> Marlene says, "Thank you for showing us, Ricca. We learned so much."

Marlene asks her staff to share a "what's working well" strategy at weekly meetings. Today, Ricca demonstrated board games. At a previous meeting, Latifa displayed a mural created by the three-year-olds. Kiara modeled a home book activity she designed for parents. Juan passed out his favorite behavior-guidance strategies.

The decision to include staff in teaching each other is a small step that creates positive change. Marlene has noticed that staff stay longer after meetings to ask each other questions. She overhears them brainstorm solutions to challenges and ask to observe one other's teaching. Marlene has a strength-based view of her staff's abilities, talents, and capacity for growth. Including staff in leading professional development has highlighted their strengths and made a big difference in their engagement.

What Works Best: Supporting Professionalism in Your Program

The following are ways that professional knowledge influences your program. Effective leaders:

- share practical knowledge and help others share their knowledge to strengthen the whole group (O'Gorman and Hard 2013);
- play a vital role in influencing the social-emotional climate of a program, which in turn impacts the experiences of staff, families, and children (Zinsser et al. 2016);
- respond and adapt to meet the needs of their community in ways that are relational; multidisciplinary; family focused; and culturally, linguistically, and economically sensitive (Nicholson and Maniates 2015);
- nurture the relational aspects of a program and take responsibility for guiding improvement processes in teaching and managing the organization to create positive growth (Sims et al. 2015);
- stay current in professional knowledge and teaching approaches and understand the needs of staff for training and support to promote positive change (Pianta 2012);
- promote professional growth in all areas of content and advocacy (Stamopoulos 2012).

Features of a healthy organization include shared adoption of your program philosophy, norms, and expectations. In relationships, staff experience consistency and mutual trust. They know that you will support them in meeting goals and will include them in decision-making processes. There is creativity in the way staff solve problems and adapt to change (Bloom, Hentschel, and Bella 2013). These interactional dynamics promote satisfaction, energy, and well-being among staff and ensure greater efficiency in achieving your goals. All of these elements are part of professionalism that will increase staff pride in their work.

The Whole Leadership Framework helps you plan training for yourself and your staff. Early childhood leaders express an urgent need to gain greater leadership expertise to train staff and teachers (Ryan et al. 2011). They view coaching, mentoring, and technical assistance as essential to help them to increase the quality of their centers, and they want support over time (Schulman et al. 2012).

You may have taken courses in program leadership, management, and administration, but leadership essentials are the driving dynamics of positive energy and change in your organization. Leadership essentials create healthy work places for children, families, and teachers. Where these dynamics are thriving, there is a spirit of collaboration lifted by a can-do attitude. Every aspect of your program is influenced by these skills, each one of which is critical for collaboration, efficacy, and creativity. Leadership essentials help you maximize the capacity of human beings who are stakeholders in your program.

When you reflect on your program, you may decide to seek training about attachment and healthy child development. You may want to learn more about the elements of high-quality care and teaching that nurture language, cognitive, social, physical, and social-emotional outcomes. In the same way, training about leadership essentials, such as knowledge of communication, conflict management, and problem solving, is a critical component of your programs' success. Your staff will benefit from learning these tools, as well.

As a director, you have the opportunity promote professional growth within your organization through on-site training. You may participate in local, state, or national professional-development opportunities. These resources can inspire, strengthen, and empower your staff to embrace learning as a natural part of teaching and care. When continuous quality improvement is your goal, there is a vital spirit of energy in daily work. The following are important avenues for professional growth.

- **Mentoring:** A mentor may be a community director with experience in supporting other programs. This person will work with you to identify needs and develop an action plan. A mentor may be one of your staff who attends training and spends time with other teachers sharing the strategies.

- **On-site consultation:** You may invite a local expert who is trained in a specific topic or an issue that is shared by your teachers. Perhaps they want to know more about literacy practices or positive guidance. An on-site consultant can help you identify goals for growth and meet the specific needs of your teaching staff or families.

- **Coaching:** A professional coach is trained in adult learning theory and specific competencies related to early childhood leadership and practice. Coaching may focus on management and business needs, teaching practices, or the relational needs of your organization. A coach will help you target specific skills or practices, set action steps for quality improvement, and offer support to reach your goals.

- **Communities of practice:** When your staff identifies an area of needed support, a community of practice is a solution. Staff can define the need; identify resources such as a study guide, book, or training video; and facilitate discussion and application. Promoting communities of practice can energize and refocus your staff. This is the perfect avenue to highlight and study leadership essentials and their importance in organizational climate and effectiveness.

- **Courses and workshops:** You and your staff may take continuing-education courses through a local university or community college or may obtain or renew your early childhood credentials.

Your ability to be a role model in ongoing learning is essential to the growth of your staff. You can demonstrate openness to positive growth and can jump-start the dynamics of learning. Modeling your own journey to gain knowledge of pedagogy and the profession will inspire and orient your staff to their own need for growth.

Take-Away Strategies: Increasing Knowledge of the Profession

As you think about action steps, what does *increasing knowledge* mean to you? What information do you need to help you achieve your goals? The following strategies will help you define your core values and get support for the next steps in your leadership journey.

- **Post your goals.** Define and aim for specific goals. Display your written goals where you can see them each day. The power of a positive purpose is transforming.

- **Embrace a growth mindset**. Growth happens with active reflection. Examine your emotions, experiences, actions, and responses in light of your core values and goals. Seek creative and constructive solutions that will move you forward. Ask yourself, "Where can minor adjustments bring about maximum change?" "How can I build the strengths of others?" "How can I shift what I am doing to create a positive impact?"

- **Find a mentor**. Ask someone you admire to share her journey with you. Learn about her goals and steps toward growth. You will gain insight, knowledge, and perspective by spending time with a more experienced colleague or early childhood professional. Learn from others who challenge you and inspire you to grow. Ask about leadership essentials and how these have impacted their program. How did they nurture and develop these in staff?

- **Promote a learning community.** Offer suggested reading materials, handouts, and other media to jump-start learning in your program. Create a monthly newsletter for staff and families to share health and wellness information, strategies for learning, positive guidance tips, and community resources. Importantly, promote the tools and competencies of leadership essentials, so that they become active and sustaining anchors for your program's vitality and success.

Leadership essentials provide the foundational competencies and individual qualities necessary for leading people that are expressed in personal leadership styles and dispositions. The tools of leadership essentials foster a healthy organizational climate, processes, and outcomes. The core dispositions flow from authentic relationships and shared mission. Leadership essentials provide a strong foundation to help you get through challenging times. They are part of a framework of resilience and optimism that can help you reorient your approach, reassess your options, and strengthen all aspects of your work.

Leadership essentials will help you bring your core values and principles to life as you honor individuals, celebrate the contributions of others, and revitalize collaboration in your program. With these tools, you will be able to influence your organization as well as expand your influence to the wider early childhood system.

⛏ Digging Deeper: Resources for Growth

The following resources can connect you to needed support, learning opportunities, and growth:

- **McCormick Center for Early Childhood Leadership:** The McCormick Center is the premier support organization for program leaders and offers many resources on Whole Leadership and related professional development. http://mccormickcenter.nl.edu/

- **Quality rating and improvement systems:** The QRIS National Learning Network has compiled a comprehensive list of QRIS contacts and websites for each state. http://qrisnetwork.org/

- **State early learning guidelines:** States have developed standards that set learning expectations for high-quality settings and that describe areas of focus needed for children at specific ages, including toddlers, English language learners, and children with disabilities or developmental delays. https://childcareta.acf.hhs.gov/sites/default/files/public/state_elgs_web_final_2.pdf

- **State departments of education:** State departments of education provide links to higher-education agencies, special-education resources, and adult-education agencies in each state. **https://www2.ed.gov/about/contacts/state/index.html**

Chapter 3 Study Guide: Putting Leadership Essentials into Practice

The whole leadership domain of leadership essentials does not stand alone. This component of whole leadership should be embedded throughout your program and program practices, along with the administrative leadership and pedagogical leadership domains. To demonstrate integration throughout a program, consider the practice of staff self-reflection on page 40. Review the list below as you consider what this practice looks like in a program where the Whole Leadership Framework is present.

- ☐ The orientation to the program and the employee handbook include information about the value of self-reflection for personal and professional growth.

- ☐ As part of orientation, staff are asked to complete questionnaires and assessments related to their previous experiences, learning preferences, strengths, leadership style, and areas for growth.

- ☐ The administrative staff use journals and forms to document ideas, thoughts, and questions related to improving operations.

- ☐ The budget includes line items for materials, such as journals for staff, to support reflective practices.

- ☐ There is a policy for pairing new staff with coaches during orientation. The coach can answer questions, challenge them, assist in their learning, and share personal experiences of overcoming struggles and accomplishing feats.

- ☐ Staff receive information about where to find a library of electronic or paper resources related to self-reflection and reflective supervision.

- ☐ Lesson-planning forms include space to write challenging questions, reflective notes, and ideas for future practice.

- ☐ Staff meetings are designed to include activities that encourage self-reflection and provide time to reflect.

- ☐ Supervisors meet regularly with those they supervise to discuss ideas and questions that arise from self-reflection.

A review of the list above depicts many ways that self-reflection is supported through administrative leadership. Can you think of additional ways self-reflection can be demonstrated through administrative leadership?

_____

_____

_____

_____

_____

Consider the ways self-reflection is supported through pedagogical leadership.

- ☐ Supervisors of teachers include self-reflection as a criterion they address during reflective supervision meetings.
- ☐ Teaching teams are configured into peer learning teams, which meet regularly, practice protocols for classroom challenges, and serve as reflection incubators.
- ☐ Staff participate in book-group discussions over lunch to learn new strategies, skills, and approaches.
- ☐ Books about self-reflection are provided to staff along with trainings related to this topic.
- ☐ After participating in a training or book reading on the topic of self-reflection, supervisors follow up with staff to discuss the experience further.
- ☐ Staff are expected to implement a practice learned from a reading or training and to discuss the outcomes with the supervisor and/or colleagues.
- ☐ Staff complete a follow-up form after attending training. The form includes a space to capture insights learned and methods for implementation.
- ☐ Once staff practice, reflect, implement, and tweak what they learn during a training, they are encouraged to present the practice and lessons learned at a meeting with their colleagues.
- ☐ Staff work with a coach who encourages self-reflection as they develop their portfolios, which are used as evidence of learning and growth during the performance-appraisal process.

A review of the list above depicts many ways that self-reflection is supported through pedagogical leadership. Can you think of additional ways self-reflection can be demonstrated through pedagogical leadership?

_____

_____

_____

_____

Review both lists above. Check the box for any example that represents a leadership essential (self-efficacy, empathy, creativity, authenticity, humility, transparency, adaptability, learning).

How else can leadership essentials be incorporated into self-reflection practices?

_____

_____

_____

Whole leadership requires the director and staff to be intentional in their actions and practices. Each domain of whole leadership is dependent on the health and functioning of the other two domains to ensure success. To be sustained, self-reflection must be supported through leadership essentials and administrative and pedagogical leadership. Administrators must consider all three components when determining a new practice.

Now you try it!

How can you improve collaboration among your staff through leadership essentials, administrative leadership, and pedagogical leadership?

- Leadership Essentials

_____

_____

_____

_____

_____

- Administrative Leadership

_____

_____

_____

_____

_____

- Pedagogical Leadership

_____

_____

_____

_____

_____

Adapted from Bella, Jill. 2016. _A Critical Intersection: Administrative and Pedagogical Leadership._ Wheeling, IL: McCormick Center for Early Childhood Leadership. Used with permission.

Maximizing Pedagogical Leadership

Pedagogical Leadership

Components of Pedagogical Leadership	Tools for Pedagogical Leadership	Effect on Organizational Health and Vitality
• **Instructional leadership:** Supporting educators in implementing curriculum • **Family engagement:** Promoting partnerships with families and fostering family leadership	• Coaching and mentoring skills • Ability to apply child-development theory and research • Knowledge of evidence-based pedagogy • Knowledge of assessment methodology • Technical credibility • Knowledge of adult learning • Family focus	• Fosters consistent program norms and expectations • Guarantees fidelity to curricular philosophy • Ensures effective use of data for evaluation and quality improvements • Optimizes learning environments

Leading the Art and Science of Teaching

Ms. Spears smiles and points, "Do you see the cocoon on the branch?"

Tommy asks, "What's the sticky stuff?"

His teacher responds, "That is a soft home for the caterpillar to rest while it turns into a butterfly. The chrysalis is spun by silk threads that come out of the caterpillar."

Several children ask, "Will it come off? Will the butterfly come out?"

Ms. Spears says, "Yes, when the butterfly is ready, it will come out of the cocoon, just like you take off your coat when you come inside. Look. Here is a tiny butterfly coming out."

Actors often describe their work as their craft, and teachers can approach pedagogy as art. Ms. Spears, a master teacher, planned this trip to the natural history museum with her class of four- and five-year-olds to see a butterfly exhibit. She provided information in advance that engaged the children's interest and helped them focus on aspects of butterflies they may not have noticed on their own. During the field trip, she guided their exploration and invited them to observe how the butterflies fly and alight on objects. She encouraged them to communicate their own ideas during the visit and when they returned to the classroom. Ms. Spears brought the curriculum to life and created a meaningful experience.

Pedagogy is both art and science. As art, you have probably observed early childhood educators who have mastered their craft and interact with children in remarkable ways to evoke wondering questions and to inspire determination for learning. For these teachers, their work is an art. They understand children and modify their practices to support learning and development. This is illustrated in a quotation by Tiziana Filippini in *The Hundred Languages of Children* (1993): "Our expectations of the child must be very flexible and varied. We must be able to be amazed and enjoy, like the children often do. We must be able to catch the ball that the children throw us and toss it back to them in ways that make the children want to continue the game with us, developing, perhaps, other games as we go along." Fostering this kind of disposition for teacher-child interactions is the heart of pedagogy as an art.

Ms. Spears prepares activities that engage children. Her words and her tone are positive and encouraging. Her classroom is carefully arranged in interest centers with beautiful materials. The shelves are labeled with words and pictures so that children can easily identify where items can be retrieved and returned. When Ms. Spears reads a book to the children, she holds it so all children can see the illustrations. She adapts the text so children can understand the story. Her tone changes with the characters, and her voice and pace capture excitement and anticipation within the written word. Her classroom promotes high-quality language through the setting and materials as well as interactions. Importantly, her pedagogical style is sensitive to the needs of the children to fully support their learning. When children struggle, Ms. Spears provides support and pairs them with others so that they can be successful. These skills exemplify the work of a teacher who has mastered the art and craft of teaching.

Ms. Spears is also an excellent technician. She has well-established systems to manage her classroom and prepares each area carefully ahead of time. She observes children's learning and documents what they say and do. She updates portfolios to show their progress over time. She communicates effectively with families and works well with assistant teachers. Each teacher carefully follows mutually understood roles and responsibilities. They carry out these tasks with consistency following a well-planned but child-centered schedule. Ms. Spears combines technical skills with the art of teaching. She knows how to use effective behavior guidance with groups of young children and how to implement systems and tasks for good teaching. This combination is the essence of great pedagogy.

Pedagogical leadership may seem like a rather academic term for early childhood education; however, it is an inclusive label to describe what early childhood teachers do to support all aspects of children's learning. Infant and toddler teachers focus on child development from a developmental perspective. They approach the growth of skills with attention to the whole child. Preschool and school-age teachers also understand the specific needs of their students. In the area of pedagogical leadership, the terms *teaching staff* and *teachers* refer to all early childhood educators and their work of nurturing and teaching young children, regardless of the setting or the ages of children of whom they serve.

As science, pedagogy involves aspects of teaching and learning based on evidence. When teachers use evidence-based methods, they can demonstrate effective practices grounded in research. For example, developmentally appropriate practice (DAP) is one of the hallmarks of our field and is extensively researched and interwoven into teaching practice. Teachers think about DAP when they arrange a classroom, interact with children, and use appropriate assessment tools. It is the science behind DAP that gives it credibility.

⚙ What Works Best: Developmentally Appropriate Practice

Pedagogical leaders must ensure that all practices in the program are developmentally appropriate. This approach affects and informs the way you set priorities and include families as informed partners in decision making. Importantly, it is the lens through which you view interactions between staff and children throughout the day in classroom settings.

DAP is an approach to teaching that is grounded in the research on how young children develop and learn and in what is known about effective early education (NAEYC 2018). The three core tenets include knowing about child development and learning, knowing what is individually appropriate, and knowing what is culturally important. Use the following resources as a guide to ensure developmentally appropriate and nondiscriminatory practices in nurturing, caring for, and teaching young children in your program.

- *Developmentally Appropriate Practice in Early Childhood Programs Serving Children from Birth through Age 8*, https://www.naeyc.org/resources/topics/dap/3-core-considerations
- *Anti-Discrimination Position Statement*, https://www.naeyc.org/resources/position-statements

---

Child observation and assessment are aspects of pedagogy that demonstrate the science of teaching. Authentic and appropriate assessment for young children may include both quantitative methods (measured in numbers) and qualitative methods (recorded in words) to capture how individual children and groups are developing. Observing children, recording and examining information, interpreting data to gain new insights, reflecting on the best ways to support growth, and adapting teaching approaches are ways that teachers apply the science of pedagogy to their work. Effective teachers observe, monitor, and assess children's skills over time so that they can adjust materials, routines, interactions, and activities to best promote learning and development.

As the leader, you influence both the art and science of pedagogy in your program. Because leadership requires motivating people, you support positive changes in all aspects of curriculum and instruction by engaging and collaborating with your staff. You work with your team and bring everyone along in the process of growth and help them carry out your philosophy, approach, and curriculum objectives.

Unifying Beliefs about How Children Learn

Director Sonja asks, "What will we do with infants and toddlers for the architecture unit?"

Patrick's mother responds, "Let's introduce a variety of soft shapes and colors. I'll create a basket of colorful shapes over the weekend from fabric scraps."

Jose's father responds, "For the toddlers, let's donate cartons and boxes to create a larger structure. The children will enjoy building with those."

Sonja encourages them, "Sounds like a great plan."

In this Reggio Emilia–inspired center, families meet monthly to brainstorm strategies to enrich learning for classroom projects. Today, the families contributed ideas about an upcoming unit on architecture. They offered their skills in photography, volunteered for a field trip, and agreed to bring in supplies for an outdoor building experience. They talked in depth about how to modify the activities for infants and toddlers and considered the best way to add increasing difficulty to challenges for older four- and five-year-olds.

A challenge for pedagogical leaders is to bring together the various beliefs and ideas of teachers, families, and other stakeholders about how children learn, so that all hold a common understanding. Shared commitment is central to developing an educational philosophy for the program, as these beliefs and approaches are translated into daily practice in the classroom. As a pedagogical leader, you must communicate consistently and engage others in carrying out your program's philosophy. Your philosophy should be much more than a narrative statement at the beginning of a parent handbook. It should be a shared understanding among stakeholders, staff, and families about the values, priorities, and approaches to learning that permeate your center's policies and practices.

The variety of early childhood philosophies and approaches is a great strength in early childhood education and are part of the rich and varied history of the profession. Families have choices as they select a program that is best for their children and fits with their values and needs. Similarly, staff may choose to work in a program that is congruent with their educational philosophy and allows them to teach in a manner that matches their interests and style.

As the pedagogical leader, you have a role in unifying the philosophy and approach adopted by the organization. For example, if your program is based on a constructivist philosophy, it is important that staff and families have a basic understanding about constructivism and how it is implemented. Philosophies and competencies should be clearly stated in the written materials, such as the staff and family handbooks; incorporated into the staff orientation process; and emphasized at ongoing staff development and family meetings. You may provide specific training to ensure that everyone in the organization understands the basic concepts of your approach and how it translates into the daily life and activities the children experience. Your responsibility is to support alignment both in classroom practices and for the organization as a whole.

As you observe in classrooms, you should see a high degree of congruence in approach, so that children experience consistency and family members sense commitment on the part of teachers to the program philosophy and goals. You will be able to evaluate whether learning experiences are consistent with the program's philosophy. The feedback you give to staff can promote open communication and foster ongoing growth and deeper application as you bring your philosophy to life. Provide opportunities to talk about how teachers approach various aspects of their work. Make sure that everyone facilitates a unifying commitment to your unique program philosophy. These conversations help foster common understanding and establish pedagogical norms.

⚙️ What Works Best: Distributed Leadership in Pedagogy

As a pedagogical leader, you share leadership functions with others in your program. While you share the vision, hire and train staff, and retain overall accountability, teaching staff take on other functions of leadership. For example, they may lead groups of teachers in preparing or reviewing lesson plans. They may lead training for a group of teachers or hold a particular area of expertise that can nurture the skills of others. They also may take on roles within the program, such as leadership with family engagement or community outreach.

Instructional leaders may provide support through various roles including resource provider, data coach, curriculum specialist, pedagogical specialist, classroom supporter, mentor, and learning facilitator (Harrison and Killion 2007). Shared responsibility through distributed leadership has been widely adopted and studied in K–12 schools (Diamond and Spillane 2016; Daly et al. 2014). Various additional staff members, such as the early childhood director or principal, a district- or multiprogram-level coordinator, a curriculum specialist, and teacher leaders may provide instructional leadership in classrooms (Abel et al. 2016). As the program leader, you provide leadership across each of these functions to coordinate the success of individuals and teams.

Exploring the Impact of Curriculum

Teacher Carolyn sits with a stuffed bear in her lap and uses an exaggerated tone to make him talk. Mr. Bear sighs and says, "I want to play with the tractor. Molly took my tractor and I wanted it." Carolyn responds to Mr. Bear with a sympathetic nod. "I can understand you feel sad, Mr. Bear." She turns to the children and asks, "What can Mr. Bear say to his friends when he wants to play with a toy?"

The children say, "He shouldn't get mad." "He should ask his friend." "He should get another tractor."

Carolyn agrees. "Those are wonderful solutions. What do you think Mr. Bear should say to his friends?"

Toby says, "He should say, 'May I play with the tractor?'"

Carolyn is a highly effective teacher and has recently introduced Mr. Bear as a member of the classroom. Carolyn skillfully uses the bear's experiences to mirror the social and emotional needs of the children. She uses the bear to help children brainstorm solutions to their dilemmas and learn to get along with others. The children are delighted to offer help to Mr. Bear and readily engage in the fantasy. Carolyn uses a variety of approaches to support the children's social-emotional learning; the bear is one effective way to help children talk about their challenges.

Curriculum includes the collective experiences of teaching that contribute to children's learning and development. Curriculum is much more than a set of materials, manuals, or a scope and sequence of content. In includes all aspects of children's experiences in your program. In early childhood settings, curriculum involves planning the environment, anticipating children's interests, and adapting the daily schedule. Curriculum also includes approaches to teaching, such as building on learning that occurred yesterday and last week and adapting learning activities to meet the needs of individual children. It also means appropriately using information gained from observation and assessment and ensuring that all practices and activities are culturally responsive and reflect the diversity of the families. As children learn during self-care routines, meals, and at nap time, positive guidance and daily interactions are also elements of curriculum in early childhood classrooms.

Your role as the program leader is to inspire excellence in the curricular program and activities throughout your organization. Effective leaders also encourage teaching staff to make autonomous curricular decisions that fit with the unique characteristics of their classroom and individual children's needs. They modify teaching strategies to meet the needs of their specific age group and setting. Your staff may use their unique abilities, passions, and skills to modify approaches, but all strive to create the highest quality setting and interactions. They may differ in some approaches, but they share a common bond that is centered in the program philosophy. This is where the art and science of teaching make a difference. It is the teacher who brings the curriculum to life.

As the pedagogical leader, you ensure that curriculum that is well-planned and thoughtfully developed. You encourage staff to motivate and inspire children to engage in classroom experiences fully. You listen and provide feedback to make sure staff know how to stimulate children's thinking and help them consider new perspectives and ways to solve problems. With younger children, you support responsive and sensitive nurturing and rich language experiences. You ensure that staff are supporting and interacting with each other to provide the highest quality setting. All aspects of curriculum are created within the social context. Your role is to provide information, resources, and support, which will result in motivation for continued growth.

⚙️ What Works Best: Zone of Proximal Development

The zone of proximal development (ZPD) is a term that represents the learning at a level just above what children can achieve independently (Vygotsky 1978). This is the level of learning that a child can achieve with the assistance of a teacher or more advanced peer. When teachers scaffold learning at the higher level of the zone of proximal development, they inspire children to dig deeper and confront challenges just beyond their capability (Berk and Winsler 1995). By transforming an activity into a more challenging task, children work collaboratively to construct knowledge and explore solutions as a group.

Supporting learning at a more complex level builds skills and encourages children to take on new and challenging problems. For example, a teacher can use questions, prompts, or cues to help children solve problems. A teacher might foster mathematical understanding by helping a child point to objects and touch each one while counting. An older or more advanced peer might demonstrate how to play a game and give the newer learner tips or help place that child's body in space. The goal is to provide increasing and individually adapted challenges with guided support to keep up with—and strengthen—the rapid skill development during the early childhood years.

🔑 Legacy of Leadership: Inspiring Responsive Teaching

"We hired new teaching staff because they had positive energy and were eager to learn. But they didn't have much experience with toddlers and needed support. We invited a social worker from the community to talk with them about attachment and why toddlers need responsive nurturing. She helped them learn effective guidance strategies. The next task we tackled was to enrich teaching. We purchased a STEM book for toddler teaching and gathered needed materials. The difference in the teachers is amazing, and all we had to do was think in new ways about what was possible."

Involving Families in Children's Learning

Classroom volunteer George laughs and points to the book illustration. "Why is the duck sitting on top of the lady's hat?" The three-year olds laugh out loud. When he turns the page, he says, "Oh my! Do you think the pig really climbed into the shopping cart?" The children giggle.

Ainsley says, "They can't put in food."

George smiles and says, "You're right, Ainsley! There is no room for groceries. The pig has taken up all the space."

Marietta and George volunteer one day each month in Ainsley's classroom. Ainsley's teacher, Patrice, values the time they take to read to children. George brings his banjo, and the children dance and sing folk songs together. Patrice has worked with families to identify their strengths and uses their talents as assets in her classroom. Patrice's director often asks her to share with other staff what she has learned about engaging families. This program encourages family involvement in classroom activities and includes families in giving feedback about the program. This program has a roster of family members who participate in classroom activities on a regular basis.

The pedagogical leader recognizes the importance of family engagement and intentionally explores ways to nurture this value with families and staff alike. As the leader in your program, you have many opportunities to influence staff and prioritize family engagement with children's learning. This approach will become part of the prevailing culture of your organization.

While chapter 6 presents a comprehensive discussion about family engagement and its benefits to children, families, and the program, it is important to understand how this priority fits within pedagogical leadership. As you develop the culture of your program, family engagement can become a meaningful reality. Your programs and initiatives and the attitudes and dispositions of staff and families will benefit from it. All must understand the benefits to children when families are involved.

As pedagogical leader, your role is to help staff recognize opportunities to collaborate and understand the reciprocal role with families to support children's learning and development. Family-engagement initiatives bring teachers and families together to create the best possible outcomes for children.

⚙ What Works Best: Building on the Strengths of Families

Because children's learning occurs in a social context, communication between families and teachers is essential (Bodrova and Leong 2007). Families can draw on their knowledge to help children make sense of new learning and challenges in the program setting. Families have a unique and valuable advantage in scaffolding children's new learning and providing needed emotional support to build knowledge (Berk and Winsler 1995). They bring essential expertise about their children to the learning equation.

Families and programs together create a fertile ground for creativity and collaboration. Successful programs embrace the strengths of families and recognize them as essential partners in current and future school success for young children. Overwhelming evidence shows the significance of involved families on the adjustment and achievement of children:

- Family engagement is especially valuable to support early literacy in linguistically diverse families (Barrueco et al. 2015).
- Family engagement increases children's age-appropriate cognitive skills and student achievement (Forry et al. 2012; Powell et al. 2010).
- Family-school partnership models emphasize the bidirectional relationship between families and schools and purport to enhance student outcomes through the development of cross-system supports and continuities across settings (Kim et al. 2012).
- Family engagement has a long-term impact on academic achievement because of the support given in the program and the values and priorities that are supported at home (Cole 2017; Wilder 2014).
- Family engagement is woven into policy and educational reforms due to its critical impact on children's short- and long-term achievement and developmental outcomes (Graves and Wright 2011).

Families represent the first essential system and source of support for children's learning and development and serve as a lifelong resource to children (Henderson and Mapp 2002). The pedagogical leader can communicate the value of family engagement by supporting, for example, literacy with diverse families, which increases children's age-appropriate cognitive skills, improves children's academic and developmental mastery, and reduces social, emotional, and behavioral problems (Roggman et al. 2009). You can influence the culture of your program by increasing awareness and knowledge of the benefits of family engagement.

Assessing Children's Development and Learning

Teacher Vonya sits quietly and watches Michael as he carefully places blocks on top of his structure. She takes digital photos during several stages of his construction and shows the pictures to him. "What kind of building is this?" she asks.

Michael answers, "I'm making a skyscraper. I putted the big towers at the top to be radio signals."

Vonya says, "Oh, you put the radio towers at the top?"

Michael answers, "Yes. They are blasting out rays to the moon."

Vonya asks, "What shall we title your photos?"

Michael says, "This is my moon ray tower."

Vonya writes down his words and points to them as she reads them back: "This is my moon ray tower."

This quiet moment between teacher and child doesn't seem much like an assessment. But this teacher is engaged in authentic assessment that suits the needs of young children. She creates a portfolio for each child at the beginning of each year. She watches the children at work and play and writes down what they do and say. Today, she writes that Michael has a rich imagination and he is very excited about the space unit. She records the book he wants to read. Next week, she will share this exciting progress with Michael's family.

Creating and implementing a plan for assessing children's growth and development is an essential leadership function that directly affects teaching and learning in the classroom. Child-centered assessment enhances the curriculum for individual children, for teachers, and for the organization as a whole. The pedagogical leader carefully considers the program's philosophy, the existing curriculum, and the perspectives and experiences of the families served in designing the assessment approaches.

NAEYC (2018) accreditation guidelines outline important factors for pedagogical leaders to consider when planning and orienting staff to child assessment:

- An assessment plan should be written and include the purpose for assessing children.
- The conditions under which the children will be assessed should be clear.
- The frequency and protocols for assessment must be defined and discussed.
- All records and information about children's records must be confidential.
- Families must be invited to contribute to the process and understand how results will be shared with them.

Child assessment uses a variety of sources to capture the change in children's progress over time. There are many tools to incorporate in your assessment plan, such as observation notes, developmental checklists, portfolios, and age-appropriate content assessments. The key is to be thoughtful about the goal of assessment. These strategies together can be used to provide a meaningful picture of children's emerging skills and can highlight areas where they can benefit from additional support.

The National Academies commissioned a report that examined the reasons for early childhood assessment (Snow and Van Hemel 2008). Assessment can be used for program evaluation, individual child development, diagnostic testing, readiness inventories, or to guide intervention and instruction. You can use information gained from carefully observing, recording, and evaluating documentation to inform shared decision making with families and other staff. For older children, curriculum products may include assessment tools that are aligned to learning objectives. For infants and toddlers, observation and assessment follow daily progress and capture milestones. These assessments can be useful for teachers as they evaluate the needs of children and ensure that learning goals are met. As a pedagogical leader, work with staff to ensure that you have chosen the best possible tools to measure progress and support the learning goals of your program.

Early screening is an important part of program responsibility and ensures that intervention needs are identified and that children receive needed supports. The Centers for Disease Control and Prevention (CDC) offers universal guidelines for children from birth through age five. You can print the milestone checklists and download the Milestone Tracker mobile app to use in your program. In addition, the CDC offers important information about early screening, early intervention, and appropriate developmental tools. For more information, see https://www.cdc.gov/ncbddd/actearly/milestones/index.html

As pedagogical leader, you make sure that the assessment plan for your program is appropriate for the children you serve and that it supports your curriculum philosophy and goals. Selected tools should be valid and reliable; bias-free in content and use; and appropriate for children from all ethnic, racial, language, and ability backgrounds. In addition, you must ensure that all classroom observations and assessments use integrated and research-based practices for children who are dual language learners. (We will discuss this in chapter 6.) The content of assessments and related materials should represent the desired domains of development you want to evaluate. In addition, materials must be used for the purpose they were intended, so that children's development is represented fairly and accurately. You and program staff may request technical support from your local school district, early intervention organizations, and funding organizations as you develop an integrated assessment plan for your program.

O—🔑 Legacy of Leadership: Using Observation to Inform Teaching

"I didn't feel I was taking leadership in the area of assessment, so I gave a form to my teaching staff. I asked them to be more intentional as they watch and listen. The form asks them to write what children say or do that shows what they understand and can do. It has a space to write strategies for support. The next space asks them to observe a child's behavior: what led up to an incident, what happened during an incident, and what happened after an incident. Staff now use this form to talk about lesson planning and behavior-guidance strategies. I wish I had done this sooner."

Using Data to Adjust Teaching and Learning Activities

Nap time has been particularly challenging. This morning, teacher Sue Ellen talks with Rae's mother. "Have you noticed changes in routine that may be affecting Rae?"

Rae's mother replies, "Well, we have a lot of company at our house. My mother is living with us. Rae is sleeping with her sister."

Sue Ellen asks, "Has this affected Rae's nighttime schedule?"

Rae's mother admits, "Yes. She has been up late."

Sue Ellen says, "Let's work together to see if we can get a more consistent routine for Rae."

Sue Ellen follows up with her director. Together, they decide to send out a family survey to evaluate sleeping hours for children and to explore the routines and strategies that families prefer for transitions to naptime. In response to the survey, and with the director's support, staff shift their approach to nap time. They modify the beginning of lunch time and add a thirty-minute transition time for soft music and reading. They assign back-patting to specific teachers, so that children experience consistency. These minor changes result in a major difference in napping routines.

Data is part of what you do every day. Understanding how to find it and use it can help you be more effective in making pedagogical decisions. You can use data to inform decisions about routines, schedules, and teaching. Over time, you can support your staff as they participate in ongoing cycles of planning, data collection, and review. Consider the following list of possible data sources that can help you understand and make decisions about learning that occurs in your program.

- Anecdotal records and written notes
- Checklists
- Observation forms
- Children's attendance records
- Lunch counts
- Incident reports
- Enrollment forms
- Purchase requisitions for classroom supplies and materials
- Classroom welcome packets
- Electronic communications to families
- Children's artwork
- Teachers' anecdotal notes
- Standardized assessment measures
- Samples of children's work
- Photographs
- Digital recordings of children
- Digital recordings of teachers
- Audio recordings

Each of these sources provides information you can use to adapt curriculum and inform teaching decisions. You may want to involve others in interpreting the data to gain different points of view and perspectives. It may be useful to have teaching teams work collaboratively on a regular basis to examine gathered data and draw conclusions about how the information can affect teaching and learning. Some data will be quantitative—number counts, frequencies, percentages—and other data will be qualitative—notes, narrative descriptions, work samples, and media. Together, these provide a well-informed picture of teaching and learning in your program.

As the program director, your role is to oversee the way teachers use, think about, and store data in all forms. The Whole Leadership Framework can help you look at all aspects of your program to decide what information you need to know. In the pedagogical leadership area, data can show you changes in an individual child's progress over time. As you consider the development of children at each age, data can help you reflect on teaching effectiveness.

Data collection can assist you in focusing priorities for professional development. For example, children can be evaluated over a specific time period to measure vocabulary and reading improvement. You can compare reading scores at the beginning and ending of a year to show overall progress. You may look carefully at social-emotional development to see what aspects of behavior guidance and emotion coaching supports can be beneficial to your teachers. You can use this information to create an action plan for improvement for the classroom and the program.

You can also use data to evaluate family engagement as part of pedagogical leadership. For example, you can compile family-survey information to see whether there are topics you want to highlight in a newsletter or invite a speaker to address. You can track attendance to see whether there are families who need additional support. You can ask families to provide feedback about events by rating quality on a 1-to-5 scale or ask open-ended questions such as, "Was this event's content helpful to your family?" "What else would you like to know?" "What would you like to see happen differently next time?" This kind of ongoing evaluation of events can offer you needed insight about your services and effectiveness with families.

Optimizing Learning Environment

Director Gia congratulates preschool teacher Benita. "I can see the way children responded differently this time. It helped so much that you provided puppets for them. They were engaged in the story. It's exciting to see the changes you have made."

Benita responds, "I was afraid to try it, thinking the children would throw them. I'm surprised at how well it worked."

In this Head Start classroom, the director and staff work together to evaluate positive improvements. They sit together after an observation and talk about the activity. Rather than feel intimidated or anxious about her director's presence, Benita is used to having Gia visit the classroom often. Sometimes Gia simply drops in to say, "Good morning." Other times, she comes to read a book to the children or to support children during activities. Once a week, she comes to spend time observing and sharing reflective conversation with Benita after the children leave. Because these patterns are consistent over time, Benita feels that Gia is a positive support and encouragement to her.

An important role of the pedagogical leader is to be a "second set of eyes" to observe the learning environment. Your program includes the physical space, the social environment, the nature and quality of staff communication, and the emotional climate of the classroom. Teachers are absorbed in their daily activities and can benefit from outside perspectives. An unbiased observer can identify opportunities teachers use to engage learning, such as teachable moments to answer children's questions or follow curiosity about a topic. At the same time, an objective observer may identify ways spaces and materials can be adapted to be more effective. For example, you may notice that children do not have enough space in the block area for ample construction play. Moving a shelf back several feet and adding additional materials can improve children's access and engagement. When this kind of feedback is shared as an ongoing and expected part of teaching, staff appreciate the supportive input. When you observe with a respectful mindset, recognizing the complex dynamics of classroom interactions, you can provide necessary support for improving pedagogy.

Early childhood technical-support specialists and coaches are an important part of ongoing quality improvement. With expert training in classroom settings and processes, they can gain a sense of the quality of an early childhood program within the first few minutes of entering a building. They can see the priorities emphasized in the program through the effectiveness of activities and content of current displays. They can gain insight about family engagement as they see positive interactions among teachers and families with children. They recognize the commitment and hard work of teaching staff by the genuine warm laughter and shared excitement about learning they observe.

Pedagogical leadership for the learning environment is particularly important when working with vulnerable children and those with risk factors, such as poverty or living within an area with community instability or violence. The quality of early childhood experiences, especially exposure to frequent conversations that stimulate language development at home and in early care settings enhances language growth and reading outcomes (Mashburn et al. 2009). In addition, early self-regulation skills, such as the ability to attend, avoid disruption, control impulses, and use planning strategies can influence future achievement (Williford et al. 2013). Self-regulation strategies require executive function skills in addition to the motivation or desire to learn (Bodrova et al. 2011; Bowes et al. 2013). Teachers can identify executive function skills and adapt materials and support strategies. As the pedagogical leader, you can support staff in recognizing this need and designing activities to foster the development of early learning skills.

⚙ What Works Best: Understanding Executive Function

Executive function, often called EF, is an emerging set of skills that include attention, memory, learning, and regulation (McCrory et al. 2010). It includes the following elements and regulatory systems:

- Attention: Intentional or self-directed focus
- Focus: Ability to filter inner and outer distractions
- Flexibility: Ability to shift attention from one activity or way of thinking to another
- Memory: Use of verbal and nonverbal working memory to hold ideas, words, and images in mind
- Regulation: Ability to choose or refrain from an action on purpose
- Energy mobilization: Ability to get started and maintain resources for a task
- Emotion competence: Ability to recognize feelings and manage responses

To incorporate support for EF, ask staff to write the steps and skills needed for planned activities. Items should include physical, verbal, social, and cognitive skills as well as EF skills. This strategy will help staff become keenly aware of the skills required for success. As the program leader, you can help staff better prepare for and support learning in more effective ways.

✏ Take-Away Strategies: Encouraging Teaching Staff

As the program leader, you have an enormous influence on the perceptions of your teaching staff. You can carry out your vision for excellence and commitment to having a lasting effect on children's development in practical ways. The following strategies will help you maximize your time and energy.

- Insert dedicated blocks of time in your calendar or planner to spend individual time with teaching staff.
- Visit classrooms on a daily basis. Even ten minutes of dedicated focus communicates to staff that your primary concern is the well-being and success of children.
- In the classroom, look for the engagement of children in activities. More than one or two children wandering or disengaged is a sign that the materials or timing need to be modified to better meet individual needs. In response, ask teachers, "How do you think the activity went?" "What did you notice about children's engagement?" "What can be modified to better engage children?"
- Look to see how development is supported in all areas. For example, do teachers provide social-emotional coaching and respond patiently to support the development of self-regulation?
- Ensure positive guidance practices along with high-expectations for all children. Watch for preparation and support for success during activities and positive redirection and encouragement during transitions.

- Listen for the use of frequent, specific, and descriptive language; meaningful conversation; and encouragement of peer interaction. Provide resources to help staff understand the importance of a language-rich environment. (See the following Digging Deeper section.)
- Encourage staff to share successful teaching strategies with each other. When a song, book, or routine goes well, ask them to record what they did and why it worked. Provide time for staff to discuss these effective strategies.

Focusing on learning dispositions such as persistence (sticking with challenging tasks) is another way to support effective pedagogy. Studies relate children's persistence with greater language and math skills (Mokrova et al. 2013). Ask teaching staff to give specific feedback to children and to narrate strategies children use to solve problems, such as, "You tried hard to fit the blocks together. You searched for another block that fit." Self-regulation, emotion competence, and social skills, along with persistence, affect ongoing achievement (McCormick et al. 2015). Attention, persistence, and achievement are highly connected (Rikoon, McDermott, and Fantuzzo 2012). For these reasons, staff should foster dispositions for learning, such as motivation and persistence, and ensure that children experience early success in the social and learning environments of each classroom.

You have a profound influence on your program's learning environment. Your influence in fostering an integrated and effective learning community is essential. Your feedback and guidance about pedagogy with staff and families are invaluable. The learning environment of your program is carried out at the classroom level, but the spirit of commitment and active growth can be seen throughout the entire program. You are the guardian of a positive culture for learning. Your pedagogical leadership fosters a community of collaboration and communication among staff and families that creates a vibrant and effective early childhood program.

⛏ Digging Deeper: Exploring High-Quality Interactions

Well-prepared settings and materials set the stage for effective teaching. Staff bring content to life by interacting and supporting children's understanding. For younger children, they stay tuned in to moment-by-moment needs and introduce objects, fingerplays, songs, and interactive games. They talk about daily experiences as they are happening. In addition to talking with children during group experiences, teachers stay active by observing, monitoring, and supporting learning during play.

Guided play, in which teachers provide increasing levels of challenge and support during child-chosen activities, is essential to young children's learning (Hassinger-Das et al. 2017). Guided play is a pedagogical tool through which children learn in conceptually rich ways and teachers are intentional and active as they foster language development and peer interaction. The following resources will help you provide leadership for a language- and literacy-rich program.

- For tools that may be used in your state quality rating and improvement system to foster high-quality teaching, see:
  - The environment rating scales at the ERS Institute webpage: https://www.ersi.info/
  - The Classroom Assessment Scoring System at Teachstone: https://teachstone.com/
- For strategies to enrich learning, language, social-emotional support, and positive guidance, see the following resources:
  - *101 Principles for Positive Guidance: Creating Responsive Teachers* (Kersey and Masterson 2012)
  - *Big Questions for Young Minds: Extending Children's Thinking* (Strasser and Bresson 2017)
  - *Big Ideas of Early Mathematics: What Teachers of Young Children Need to Know* (Erikson Math Collaborative 2013)
  - *Let's Talk Toddlers: A Practical Guide to High-Quality Care* (Masterson 2018)
  - *Powerful Interactions: How to Connect with Children to Extend Their Learning* (Dombro, Stetson, and Jablon 2011)
  - *The Intentional Teacher: Choosing the Best Strategies for Young Children's Learning* (Epstein 2007)
- For family partnerships to enhance learning, language, and social-emotional development, see:
  - *Enjoying the Parenting Roller Coaster: Nurturing and Empowering Children through the Ups and Downs* (Masterson and Kersey 2016)

See chapter 6 to learn more about guiding program professional development and continuous quality improvement.

Chapter 4 Study Guide: Exploring Pedagogical Leadership

Reflecting on the Art and Science of Leadership

Teaching is described as both an art and a science. Chapter 4 provides examples of how teachers approach teaching through these two lenses. Complete the following phrases:

- Pedagogical leadership is like art because

_____

_____

- Pedagogical leadership is like science because

_____

_____

Think about your pedagogical leadership style. Do you approach leading staff like an art? If so, describe how this is done.

_____

_____

_____

_____

_____

Think about your pedagogical leadership style. Do you approach leading staff like a science? If so, describe how this is done.

_____

_____

_____

_____

_____

Reflect on your responses above. Do you favor art or science in your pedagogical leadership style? Explore the list of strategies below and check two you would like to try with your staff.

Pedagogical Leadership as an Art	Pedagogical Leadership as a Science
☐ Intentionally prepare for teacher observations by relating the observations to teachers' goals or letting teachers determine the purpose of the observation in advance.	☐ Observe various formats teachers use to document development and learning.
☐ Intentionally prepare for reflective-supervision meetings by creating an agenda in advance, determining the purpose and desired outcomes, and/or selecting examples from observations that support points you want to highlight.	☐ Review your observation notes, and interpret the information from different perspectives.
☐ Establish the best ways to encourage a staff member by considering what type of feedback this person responds best to and reflecting on the words you will use in conversation and your tone of voice.	☐ Embed information from teacher observations into feedback meetings.
☐ After classroom observations, make connections between what you observed and children's responses.	☐ Use information from mutually established goals to guide observations, conversations, and resource choices.
☐ Ask questions to elicit self-reflection and new learning.	☐ Compare observations over time, looking for changes and trends.
☐ Share resources that enhance skills needed for improvement with staff.	☐ Modify reflective-supervision meetings based on new data you gather from teachers.
☐ Take advantage of spontaneous opportunities to scaffold learning.	☐ Determine what information is needed to scaffold ongoing teacher learning.
☐ Intentionally plan meetings to elicit behaviors and actions.	

Pedagogy: A Link among Organization, Teachers, and Family

Pedagogical leadership is as relevant for families as it is for teachers. How do you address various beliefs, ideas, and practices about child rearing and learning among your staff and families? For example, do you involve families in discussions or activities about the curriculum or methods of teaching? Provide examples of what you and your teachers have done to bridge various beliefs, ideas, and practices.

_____

_____

_____

The Role of the Pedagogical Leader in Curriculum Development

As a pedagogical leader, your role includes ensuring that the curriculum contributes to children's growth and development. What do you do now, and what will you do in the future with your teachers to encourage a well-planned and thoughtfully developed curriculum?

Pedagogical leadership, like leadership essentials and administrative leadership, takes time to implement. Assess how much time you currently spend on pedagogical leadership tasks by completing the chart below.

Pedagogical Leadership Tasks	Hours Spent Per Week
Observing staff	
Reviewing teacher documents or video clips related to pedagogical topics	
Meeting one-on-one with staff to provide feedback	
Meeting with teaching teams to provide feedback	
Meeting with teaching teams to provide training	
Meeting with the entire staff to provide feedback and/or training	
Reading books, journals, other resources on pedagogical topics for your knowledge	
Reading books, journals, other resources on topics to support areas staff are working on improving	
Attending professional development on pedagogical topics	
Facilitating discussions about children's data to make decisions	
Helping create an IPDP with staff	
Creating and facilitating peer learning groups	
Other:	
Other:	
Other:	
Total number of hours per week spent on pedagogical tasks:	

After totaling the number of hours per week spent on pedagogical tasks, determine whether you would like to spend more or less time on this whole leadership component.

☐ More time

☐ Less time

If you would like to spend more time on pedagogical leadership, what needs to happen to accomplish your goal? Will you need to make structural changes, shift some responsibilities, delegate tasks to others, or prioritize in a different way? Write specific action steps below.

_____

_____

_____

_____

_____

_____

_____

_____

_____

_____

_____

Using Tools for Pedagogical Leadership

Tools for Pedagogical Leadership

- Applying child-development theory and research
- Coaching and mentoring skills
- Knowledge of evidence-based pedagogy

- Knowledge of assessment methodology
- Technical credibility
- Knowledge of adult learning
- Family focus

Applying Child-Development Theory and Research

Charise, the program director, consults with Ira and Amita, teachers in the preschool classrooms. Amita says, "We had a great reading time today. We played the word-rhyming game, and the children loved it. We had a letter hunt in the classroom. Ira helped me create the letter tags and place them around the room. After reading the story, we wrote the vocabulary words and the children were able to identify the beginning consonants. I was so excited to see the children's response."

Ira adds, "In my room, we added pictures to our word wall. The children drew the illustrations. Come and see."

These teachers are excited to see the changes in children's learning. Charise recently attended a professional-development conference at which she learned new insights about emergent literacy. When she returned, she shared information from the conference during a lead teachers meeting. She provided information about literacy skills, such as phonological awareness, knowledge of the alphabet, print awareness, vocabulary building, comprehension, and story grammar. Then she asked teacher leaders of the program's professional learning communities (PLC) to focus on one specific strategy and find out what the current research could tell them. Each PLC leader prepared a brief presentation and shared a strategy. Ira and Amita are two teachers who used the strategies. Charise works with them to document and evaluate the positive changes.

Pedagogical leaders must have a deep understanding of child-development theory and stay informed about new research that can improve their practice. Charise stays informed about current issues in early literacy by attending conferences and exploring an issue she knows she needs to address in her program. She takes the initiative to lead teaching staff through a process that deepens their understanding, as well. By sharing the leadership responsibility for this activity with teacher leaders, they become invested in the content and in creating positive results by working in learning communities. Teachers become committed to new practices. As a result, they worked with their director to conduct *action research*, an evidence-based technique to collect data and evaluate the effects of changes on children's learning. These processes lead to vitality and engagement, as well as ongoing cycles of learning and growth. Charise's leadership in guiding the needed area of growth adds to the success of the initiative.

Your professional growth as a pedagogical leader is essential to the way child-development theory and emerging research contribute to the effectiveness of your program. Just like the need for alignment of a curriculum and program philosophy, teaching and learning need to be aligned with evidence to be effective. Ensuring that your program's teaching and learning is consistent with developmental theory and research is essential to creating a high-quality setting.

⚙️ What Works Best: Using Implementation Science for Curriculum Review

All programs should maintain a current, written curriculum plan, including manuals, handbooks, lesson plans, concept maps, and theme schedules. These items can be used to discuss goals and plans with families as well as staff. Your program plan should be written into the program's philosophy, guiding documents for teachers, and fluid working documents that can guide curriculum development.

Your plan should include a positive discipline policy and related strategies, as well as respectful approaches to self-care and nurturing routines. If you use published curriculum books or kits, these are considered as tools that your teachers use to create curriculum. The way teachers interact with children to foster development, language, and learning are essential parts of your curriculum plan. Consult your state's early learning guidelines for appropriate learning goals and age-appropriate strategies for teaching.

Implementation science provides an effective tool for examining the effectiveness of your curriculum. It is a cycle of learning, reflection, and execution that can improve teaching effectiveness and be used for your program's curriculum-review process. Implementation science provides a feedback structure to help you evaluate practices and take steps for improvement. In this context, *implementation* refers to all aspects of your curriculum, which are reflected in your written plan (Fixsen et al. 2005).

The stages for using implementation science are exploration, preparation, implementation, and sustainment (Goldstein and Olszewski 2015). In the example above, Charise's program implemented new literacy approaches using these stages:

- **Exploration:** PLC conversations and investigation of research to identify effective strategies
- **Preparation:** Staff presentations and discussions about applying new practices
- **Implementation:** Trying out new practices in teaching and evaluating their effectiveness
- **Sustainment:** As Charise and the staff incorporate new literacy practices into their curriculum, they begin to dive deeper by adding new books, involving families, and continuing to improve over time.

During each part of the cycle, both informal and formal evaluations are conducted. Stakeholders, including teaching staff, specialists, and families, can provide input before moving on to the next phase. Cycles may be repeated when evaluation or feedback suggest that additional changes are needed.

Ensuring that current child-development theory and research is understood and applied in your program will include a systematic and comprehensive review of your curriculum. Evaluate all aspects of curriculum for the ages you serve. This task can be made easier by using guidance provided in NAEYC's accreditation standards. This authoritative reference includes eleven topic areas:

- Essential Characteristics
- Social and Emotional Development
- Physical Development
- Language Development
- Early Literacy
- Early Mathematics
- Science
- Technology
- Creative Expression and Appreciation for the Arts
- Health and Safety
- Social Studies

Each area provides a definition and recommended best practices. As you and your staff explore these items in detail, this resource will provide valuable insights to improve your curriculum and ensure that you consider all areas of development and learning in a comprehensive program. You can find it as a downloadable pdf on the NAEYC website.

Understanding Evidence-Based Teaching

Alba talks with her director, "I get excited when teachers ask me about next steps. We've worked to improve the play areas and provide more resources and books. Now we're talking about facilitating social-emotional learning. We just got a set of puppets and designed new lesson plans."

Lindsey responds, "That's terrific. Let's see what else we can find on the CASEL* website. They have terrific resources about evidence-based social and emotional learning."

Alba was recently promoted from teaching in the four-year-old room to assistant director in an independent child care center. One of her primary responsibilities is to observe in the classrooms and provide feedback to the teachers to improve their practice. While she feels confident in her own teaching abilities, she wants to be sure all teachers are using best practices. She wants her feedback to be based on research.

*Collaborative for Academic, Social, and Emotional Learning

⚙️ What Works Best: Using Teaching Practices with Impact

While many educators intuitively make teaching choices, it is essential to align practice with research to be sure daily choices actually have a positive effect on children's learning. The following are pedagogical levers—approaches to teaching that influence and predict positive child outcomes.

- **Social-emotional responsiveness:** Warm and emotionally responsive relationships with children in settings with consistent and stable routines foster positive behavior and learning outcomes (Buettner et al. 2016). Teacher responsiveness includes the ability to anticipate, support, and follow through with positive and effective behavior guidance. These practices are associated with positive emotional, behavioral, and cognitive child outcomes (Denham et al. 2013; Thomason and La Paro 2013).

- **Stress management:** Children need ongoing support to manage stress and to solve problems. Teachers must first manage their own stress through self-awareness, self-compassion, and mindfulness to be able to model resilience and needed skills (Jennings et al. 2014). The ability to regulate stressful experiences affects the quality of the emotional bond between children and teachers. A secure attachment relationship supports children's well-being, overall development, and learning (Commodari 2013).

- **Classroom process quality:** Classroom management skills, appropriately stimulating learning activities, and responsiveness to children have a positive effect on child outcomes (Mashburn et al. 2008). Teachers must provide explicit social, emotional, physical, and instructional support to foster learning, which leads to increased cognitive skills and social-emotional development (Jeon et al. 2016).

- **Cognitive stimulation:** Teachers must promote children's thinking and problem solving by engaging them in increasingly complex learning. By using ongoing scaffolding and feedback loops to promote concept development, teachers can help children to engage in progressively higher levels of learning over time (Booren et al. 2012; Chien et al. 2010). This approach includes efforts by teachers to promote active engagement throughout the day during teacher-directed instruction, child-initiated activities, play-based activities, routines, outdoor play, and meals (Goble et al. 2016; Goble and Pianta 2017).

- **Language and literacy facilitation:** Children need to hear rich language; participate in meaningful back-and-forth conversations; engage in positive peer interactions; and develop language to express ideas, ask for help, ask questions about learning, and explain their understanding (Conn-Powers 2013). Children use language to develop critical-thinking skills and self-regulation and to engage in complex reasoning (Whittaker and McMullen 2014). Teachers need to support language concepts and vocabulary and to foster literacy across content areas (Luna 2017).

Continued on page 84

Continued from page 83

- **Self-regulation and executive function supports:** Specific support for self-regulation, such as increasing self-management of emotions and the body, and the skills of executive function, such as keeping information in mind, directing attention, and inhibiting or activating behavior when needed, predict children's ability to productively engage in and experience greater academic achievement over time (Fitzpatrick and Pagani 2011). Executive-function skills affect planning, organization, flexibility, and the ability to organize behavior to reach goals, skills which are predictive of school achievement (De Franchis et al. 2017).

- **Positive attitude and self-efficacy:** A teacher's ability to remain calm, warm, and responsive in spite of daily stress or challenges affects both interactions with children and teaching quality (Hall-Kenyon et al. 2014). Because teachers must manage job-related challenges, participate in meaningful professional development, and manage their own personal wellness, the ability and motivation to seek help and support is critical (Jeon et al. 2018).

- **Active play:** Program leaders need to foster understanding among staff about the developmental need of children for active play. Hirsh-Pasek et al. (2015) explain that children need ample time during each day for exercise and self-directed play that is active, engaged, meaningful, and socially interactive.

Digging Deeper: Resources for Evidence-Based Curriculum

Evidence-based pedagogy is an important part of early childhood teaching. Before you purchase materials, be sure to explore evidence that shows the approach is effective. Standards for early childhood education should be evidence based just as in other educational sectors (Purper 2016). If a pedagogical method is suggested in professional development or through commercial vendors, you should first check to see if it meets research-based criteria.

Several federally funded organizations list evidence-based curricula as a starting point for your exploration. First, consult with the office of early childhood education in your state department of education to look for recommended print curricula. In addition, explore research evidence that is documented in the materials you review. The following resources can get you started:

- Center on the Social and Emotional Foundations for Early Learning (CSEFEL) is funded by the Office of Head Start and the Child Care Bureau. Content on this site focuses on social and emotional development.

- Early Childhood Technical Assistance Center (ECTA) is funded by the Office of Special Education Programs (OSEP) and offers information on an array of topics related to early childhood pedagogy.

- What Works Clearinghouse (WWC) is operated by the Institute of Education Sciences. It includes a section dedicated to early childhood education.

Ensuring Bias-Free Curriculum and Assessment

Loretta, director of a large early childhood program, overhears Isabella and Olivia, teachers of three-year-olds, talking. Olivia says, "I was so concerned about getting families to conferences, but our new strategies worked. Instead of making everyone come at the same time, we spread out options over several weeks. We also invited children to come with their parents, so child care would not be a problem."

Isabella says, "I decided to visit two families at home, instead of having them come here. The older daughter was able to translate for us, and I learned so much about the family. I wish I had thought to do that before. Before I went, I didn't realize how much the children benefit from their families. They have such close-knit relationships."

Loretta works as a director for a national child-care organization. Her program is located in a large metropolitan area. The community is rapidly becoming more diverse, with many dual language learners. The national organization has a strong commitment to multicultural education and offers training to support staff in bias-free and culturally responsive practices.

Loretta has been working for months to encourage her staff to understand the strengths of families. Shifting family-conference policies was part of raising awareness of the needs of families. Together, the staff have talked about their own social, cultural, and language experiences. This has been meaningful, as staff have shared personal instances of feeling excluded or misunderstood. They have talked about the values of the program as being fully inclusive and bias-free in its practices.

For the program leader, a critical priority is to foster a bias-free culture. It means holding the highest expectations and ensuring children have needed supports for success. Viewing curriculum evaluation and child assessments through a multicultural lens will help you ensure a bias-free environment. Bias-free teaching addresses the factors that affect learning, including communication, planning, and critical reflection (Kuh et al. 2016). Teachers need to be sensitive to families that understand the curriculum or socialize language development in differing ways. Hidden values or challenging expectations, such as finding child care to participate in family conferences, may be barriers to feeling fully welcome and accepted in a program.

A culturally and linguistically responsive curriculum makes instructional adaptations, incorporates home experiences, and uses materials that reflect the languages and cultures of all families. For dual language learners, supportive positive relationships with teachers are crucial. Children thrive in language-rich classrooms with meaningful learning experiences and benefit from strong partnerships between teachers and families (Gillanders, Castro, and Franco 2014; Massing et al. 2013). Assessment approaches should be authentic, informal, ongoing, and embedded in the daily activities the children regularly encounter. As pedagogical leader, your role is to ensure that teachers use culturally and linguistically responsive practices that build the strengths of all children.

Effecting change to eliminate bias within an organization is essential. The following steps can help you talk with staff about practical ways to shift mindsets and create strong connections for all families.

- Recognize that biases exist and engage in open conversation to promote understanding.
- Gain collective commitment among staff to create a bias-free environment.
- Create initiatives to provide professional development and create bias-free practices in all aspects of program systems.
- Establish organizational norms that include ongoing reflection and evaluation.
- Include family feedback to foster open communication and remove barriers.
- Evaluate assessment approaches for content, methods of child interaction, expectations, and support for success.
- Provide materials and resources for ongoing self-study about bias-free practices for community of practice learning among staff.

⛏ Digging Deeper: Resources for Bias-Free Programs

- *Leading Anti-Bias Early Childhood Programs: A Guide for Change* by Louise Derman-Sparks, Debbie LeeKeenan, and John Nimmo (2015). This practical guidebook provides a framework to leading an organization along a journey toward a bias-free program.
- *Narrative Inquiry in a Multicultural Landscape: Multicultural Teaching and Learning* by JoAnn Phillion (2002). This book offers a critical perspective through storytelling of how bias can be embedded in educational settings.
- "Curriculum and Assessment Considerations for Young Children from Culturally, Linguistically, and Economically Diverse Backgrounds" by Linda Espinosa (2005). This article in *Psychology in the Schools* provides comprehensive and detailed strategies to build children's competence.

Motivating Change with Adult Learning Principles

Director Noriko has been leading her program for sixteen years and enjoys working to help classroom teachers to improve their skills. She talks with Winona, a teacher in a three-to-five-year-old mixed-age classroom. "Winona, I enjoyed taking notes during my observation. I loved how you talked with Enrique and Dallas in the block center this morning. You asked them about the smokestacks and elevator in the factory they were building. They were so excited to explain it to you!"

Winona smiles and replies, "Yes. I think I am getting better at talking with children during play."

Noriko asks, "What was your reason for choosing to comment on the building?"

Noriko uses adult learning strategies to motivate Winona. First, she offers positive, specific feedback as she describes the details of the interactions between Winona and the children. This type of feedback with adults is effective because it is specific and constructive and occurs directly after the observation.

Noriko also asks the critical question, "What was your reason for choosing . . . ?" Critical questions encourage teachers to evaluate practice on a high level of cognitive processing that is intentional and proactive (Isik-Ercan and Perkins 2017). The environment is safe because Noriko has framed the critical question in a way that is objective. There is not a right or wrong answer. In her own way, Winona can explain how she was intentional using powerful interactions with the children (Dombro et al. 2011).

Adult learning theory emerged from the organizational-development field and was introduced for education by Malcom Knowles (1984). He recognized that adult learners are different from other students in that they are self-directed, come with a foundation of experiences, are ready to learn, and are task motivated. Adult learning principles will help you be effective in your interactions with staff and will motivate them to grow as individuals and teachers.

0—🔑 Legacy of Leadership: Thriving in the Role of Pedagogical Leader

"I thought my teachers were magic with children. They all had so much more experience in the classroom than I did. I didn't know if they would view me as a support, as my background is in business management. But I began spending time in the classroom and really getting to know them and their teaching approaches. I learned a lot and began reading to children. When they saw me interacting with families and children, they gained respect. I had to overcome my fear and grow into my role as a pedagogical leader."

Building Coaching and Mentoring Skills

Coach Johnna says, "Catrice, I did a simple tally of your interactions with the children during the free-play time. You interacted so much more today. I can see you're improving the balance between boys and girls. You reached out to Kia to include her in play. She was one of the quieter children we identified during my last visit."

Catrice replies, "Thanks. It helps that you come in, because then I think more intentionally about the way I interact with the children."

Johnna is an instructional coach for a school district and supports teachers' pedagogy with job-embedded professional learning experiences. She works with teachers to identify areas of strength. She also identifies areas for growth and creates professional development plans to improve their practice.

During previous visits, Catrice and Johnna decide to work on teacher-child interactions to increase the frequency and quality of conversations. They develop a coaching plan to address these needs with a specific focus on the frequency of interactions.

Coaching as pedagogical leaders means guiding individuals by challenging them and supporting them to achieve their professional objectives. Like Johnna, coaches work with teachers to support them in identifying needs, developing action plans, and scaffolding professional development.

Consistent with adult learning principles, coaches work with teachers to self-identify areas for development. Self-determination—the control of decision-making and focus—is a cornerstone of coaching relationships.

In contrast to a coach, a mentor is often a more capable peer from within an organization, rather than a specialist from outside the organization. The principles of adult learning are foundational within organizations, as well.

As a pedagogical leader you may be serving in a coaching role like Johnna, or you may coach teachers as their supervisor. In both circumstances, teachers need to feel autonomy in decision making and in determining their professional goals for growth. Using adult learning approaches can help you be more effective as a role model and coach, as you build relationships and encourage your teaching staff.

Demonstrating Technical Credibility

During nap time, preschool teacher Mitchell talks about his new director, Lawanda, with his colleagues. "I am surprised how open she is to feedback about changes I suggested for the center's curriculum. I figured since she has a master's in instructional design, she would dictate how things were going to go. I showed her some of the plans we hoped to carry out in our classroom, and she encouraged us to do it. She asked me to put together a proposal for implementing the reading strategies center-wide. Lawanda said we could work together on rolling it out to the rest of the staff."

Technical credibility is your ability to demonstrate competencies to your staff. It affects the way others perceive your competence as a leader. They form perceptions from your demonstrated knowledge, technical skill, and depth of judgement about early childhood pedagogy and learning.

Lawanda demonstrates technical credibility through her educational background and the thoughtful approach she takes when Mitchell wants to share innovative practices for the classroom. It is apparent to Mitchell that Lawanda is an expert in curriculum and instruction. It is her response about including her as a collaborative partner that motivates him to drive his ideas forward. She has a mentoring disposition that accepts teachers as developing people and professionals. She takes on a helping posture and seeks to understand situations from the perspectives of the teachers.

The relationship between technical credibility and a mentoring disposition is key to effecting change as a pedagogical leader. Leadership is based on relationships and the way staff perceives you in your role. The respect and inclusiveness you show reflects both technical ability and a mentoring disposition. This combination affects how staff respond when you introduce needed change. The chart on the next page shows how teachers respond to pedagogical support in various combinations of these two dimensions.

Teacher Perceptions of Pedagogical Support

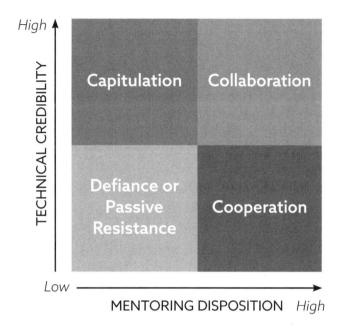

Mitchell's experience with Lawanda illustrates the ideal with high technical credibility and a high mentoring disposition, which leads to collaboration.

High Technical Credibility + High Mentoring Disposition = Collaboration

If you do not have a background that leads to high technical credibility, you can still be an effective pedagogical leader. You can make positive change happen by gaining the cooperation of the staff and building on the collective strengths of the group. Acknowledging that you are not an expert can actually increase your credibility rather than diminish it, if you are willing to approach pedagogical decisions with humility and a learner's spirit.

Low Technical Credibility + High Mentoring Disposition = Cooperation

Classroom teacher Lucile comments, "My director, Aline, comes in my classroom every day. She is always a support. Sometimes she talks with me about a child's behavioral issue. Sometimes she comes in a leadership role. She always makes herself available for questions, comments, and needs—anything that pops up."

Even when you feel stretched thin with administrative and pedagogical responsibilities, demonstrating that you are accessible to staff is an important part of leadership. Lucille perceives that Aline is available to her and willing to work with on pedagogical issues on a daily basis. Because Lucille perceives Aline to have a mentoring disposition, she is willing to cooperate and feels good about the relationship.

You may have high technical credibility, but this must be paired with a mentoring disposition to strengthen your leadership. Teachers need to know that you understand the challenges they face and that their perspective and ideas matter. You may have the knowledge and skills for excellent pedagogy, but staff may only capitulate or respond by conceding to your direction because you are the boss.

> High Technical Credibility + Low Mentoring Disposition = Capitulation

Daria complains, "Melissa doesn't understand what is happening here. She comes in and tries to direct how we do things, but she can't just turn this into an academic program to make her look good. We just go along with it to keep from ruffling her feathers."

The most detrimental situation occurs when staff perceive that the pedagogical leader is not technically credible and also does not demonstrate a mentoring disposition. Even if other elements of the program, such as using evidence-based curricula, instituting well-designed environments, and implementing effective systems for program administration, are strong, when there is a combination of low technical credibility and a low mentoring disposition, staff will resist program changes either in a passive manner or through outright defiance.

> Low Technical Credibility + Low Mentoring Disposition = Defiance or Passive Resistance

Understanding the dynamics of leadership through technical credibility and a mentoring disposition can have a profound effect on your pedagogical leadership and organizational climate. Consider the daily moments you have to influence the perceptions of staff. How do you react to their ideas? How do you present information from your knowledge base? How do you respond when they have a need? The old adage, "People don't care what you know until they know that you care," applies to the foundational need for technical credibility.

Chapter 5 Study Guide: Putting Pedagogical Leadership into Practice

Using Data in Lesson Planning

Read the following scenario and complete the activity.

> Deidre, the director at Early Explorers Early Care and Education Center, expresses her frustration with teaching staff in her program who complain about having to do quarterly assessments of children. Deidre's coach, Corinna, asks her to describe the situation further. Deidre tells her that during multiple staff meetings, teachers complain that it seems as if they are assessing the children all the time. Right when they finish doing assessments they feel they have to start them again to meet the quarterly deadlines. These frustrations are also expressed by several teachers during individual reflective supervision meetings.
>
> Deidre is especially concerned that the information gleaned from the assessments is not being used in lesson planning. Corinna asks Deidre whether there are policies in place that describe the assessment and lesson-planning process. She also asks Deidre to describe how the staff are oriented and trained to conduct the assessments, analyze the data, and incorporate it into their work with children.
>
> Next, Corinna asks Deidre what structures are in place to support the teachers to accomplish this admittedly lengthy task. She asks Deidre to reflect on the individual learning needs, strengths, and experiences of each teacher and how these are related to assessment completion. In addition, Corinna asks whether staff are able to make meaning of the assessment results and link the information to classroom activities.
>
> Deidre recognizes that teachers need more support. She wants staff to feel competent and be successful over time. This conversation sparks further exploration about how she can better support teachers with a whole leadership perspective. Corinna uses the following activity to help Deidre reflect further and create new supports to ensure that the practice of using data in lesson planning will be effective.

Using the scenario above, and drawing on your own program experience overseeing the practices and use of child-assessment data to improve teaching, answer the following questions.

Leadership Essentials

- How confident are you in your ability to explain, orient, coach, and supervise staff on child assessment practices?

- In what ways do you consider individual learning needs, such as learning approaches, personality type, and teaching strengths, in your approach with providing feedback and support to the teacher(s)?

- Are you able to relate to and share similar concerns as the director in the scenario above? If so, describe your circumstances.

- Are there creative solutions to achieve effective child documentation and assessment? Are there other ways to incorporate assessment, such as observation notes, developmental checklists, and portfolios?

- Do you have full disclosure related to procedures and purposes for child observation, documentation, screening, and assessment? Are teachers informed of everything they need to know to successfully accomplish these tasks?
- Can the current procedures for documenting children's progress be adapted? If so, how will you communicate with staff that there is a possibility for changes?

Administrative Leadership

- What policies should be included in new-employee orientation to support staff competency in strength-based child observation, documentation, screening, and assessment, and in the use of data in communication and teaching?
- What activities should be included in new-employee orientation to support staff competency in strength-based child observation, documentation, screening, and assessment, and in the use of data in communication and teaching?
- Is the use of observation, written records, checklists, and other assessments addressed at team meetings? If so, in what other ways can you encourage commitment, understanding, and competence?
- What evidence is displayed that shows the priority of accurate documentation of children's progress over time? Can this be seen in posted materials, and is it visible in behaviors, conversation, and language?
- How do you support child assessment and screening, along with related materials and training for staff, in your program budget?
- What barriers do you face to better supporting staff training and effectiveness?

Pedagogical Leadership

- Are staff informed how their assessment practices relate to the program's mission, vision, and curriculum?
- Do staff have resources to learn about or supplement their learning in the area of assessment?
- Do staff supervisors observe teaching staff and review completed documents for the purpose of providing feedback on assessment practices?
- Do staff supervisors include coaching, self-reflection activities, and resources about child assessment in reflective supervision meetings?
- Have you encouraged peer learning teams to learn collaboratively about child assessment? Is there paid time built into the day for this practice to occur?
- Have you provided materials, resources, and professional-development opportunities related to effective child assessment?
- Is there a forum for practicing information learned during professional-development experiences? If so, is there a procedure for staff to receive observation and feedback on implementation?
- Do staff observe and mentor one another as they practice child-assessment approaches?
- Is competency in child assessment listed on staff job descriptions?
- Is using data in lesson planning included in criteria on performance appraisal forms?
- Do the assessment tools, observational notes forms, and lesson planning forms lend themselves to capture needed information efficiently?
- Are families aware of screening and assessment practices through individual conversations, family meetings, program policies, and the family handbook? In what ways could families be more involved in child assessment processes?

Encouraging Family Engagement

Building Bridges between Home and School

Vanya brings her ten-month-old daughter and two-year-old son, Taylor, into the infant room where teacher Mrs. Hedley greets them with a warm smile and hug. "Smells like cinnamon in here!" Vanya says.

Mrs. Hedley agrees. "Yes. We are having smelly fun today in all of the classrooms." She points to Taylor's nose and says, "Do you smell the cinnamon, too?" He smiles back at her.

Vanya gives one last hug and kiss to her daughter and takes Taylor's hand. "Let's go see what's smelly in your classroom today."

Vanya and Roekel have just moved to the city. Both work full time and wanted to find an early childhood program close to their work location. They hoped for a place where they could be involved, an extension of their lives that would feel like a close community. They wanted their children to feel that the center was like extended family. They were drawn to this program because of the "Coffee and Conversation" events held every other week for families. They immediately established friendships with other parents and felt relieved to be welcomed as active participants in program planning and activities.

The bulletin boards outside each classroom host family photos with the caption, "My dream for my child is . . ." Responses printed under the family photos include, "My dream is for Rhonda to be brave, kind, and compassionate." "My dream for Taylor is for him to go to college and develop his talents." "My dream for Arianna is to be caring and make a difference in the world."

These photos and comments do much more than reflect the faces of families. They instill recognition that all families share hopes and dreams and are invested in the quality of children's early experiences. Even more, the photos show that members of a program need each other and are part of the same mission and goals. Above the display, a banner says, "Building strong children, families, and communities for a bright future." This message promotes optimism and unity and infuses a spirit of understanding between staff and families. Children point up as they enter and leave each classroom and say, "There we are. Look, Daddy. It's me."

In this diverse community, some families live in the neighborhood, and others commute to work here. The community is undergoing renewal as younger families move to be closer to jobs.

This program has a Community Café, a room where coffee and conversations draw families together. Families donate treats and place a few dollars in a container to fund the project. Many kinds of families are here: single parents, grandparents, multiple generations living together, and diverse racial and cultural family groups. All are engaged in the same purpose: fostering a network of support for their children to thrive.

Family engagement is an important aspect of pedagogical leadership. Not only is family communication necessary for classroom care and teaching practices, but families also contribute to the vitality and productivity of the center itself. Your role in promoting strong family partnerships includes connecting with and getting to know families well. As a result, you will be able to maximize the talent and resources of families as partners in the many priorities and activities of your program.

What Works Best: Collaborating with Families

Family engagement is a strength-based perspective that recognizes the importance of family participation in children's learning and well-being (Halgunseth 2009). It involves participation in open communication, shared decision making, reciprocal exchange of knowledge, coordination of learning between home and school, and collaboration in establishing goals (Epstein 2001). Setting up an open and positive system of communication creates productive teacher-family relationships and ensures a strong bridge between home and school (Kersey and Masterson 2009).

Positive engagement offers many benefits to children and families. When family members are involved in supporting development and learning, children experience greater social and emotional development along with increased achievement and success in school (Christenson and Reschly 2010; Larocque et al. 2011; Van Voorhis et al. 2013). Active involvement transforms family life when parents participate in reading, language, and literacy experiences (Stoltz et al. 2015). For children with special needs, close collaboration ensures full integration and success (Ancell et al. 2018). Early school involvement connects families with support services and ensures a successful transition for children from the early years to kindergarten (Stein et al. 2013).

Family engagement benefits teaching staff, as well. Through ongoing interaction, staff learn about the unique needs of children, their community and cultural experiences, and their language needs. As a result, teachers can individualize and enrich care and learning (Virmani, Wiese, and Mangione 2016). For children who are dual language learners, family involvement provides needed knowledge to foster sensitivity and understanding (Fort and Stechuk 2008). Family involvement produces a program that is welcoming and inclusive and that shapes children's and families perceptions of schools as a positive resource and support (Nitecki 2015).

The Whole Leadership Framework prioritizes the work of family engagement. As the leader, you oversee staff development related to their collaboration with families. You connect families and children to community resources. Most of all, you model authentic relationship building with individual families and look for opportunities to serve and strengthen their lives. As they provide feedback and participate in the life of your program, you—and they—are rich beneficiaries.

Ensuring Culturally Responsive Practice

> Director Freda talks with the kitchen staff. "We appreciate the soup. The toddlers enjoyed the *posole* and loved the *bolillos*. They ate every crumb. I am glad we could do this for them."
>
> Sarina responds, "We are glad when our babies are happy."

When the teaching staff let Freda know the toddlers were not responding well to the menu, she took action. She asked families to respond to a brief survey about the foods they are eating at home. As a result, Freda asked the cook to include some of the flavors and dishes families enjoy at home. The results have been terrific. Not only do the toddlers enjoy the food, but families appreciate the opportunity to work with kitchen staff to modify recipes.

Culture impacts ways of communication, meal traditions, religious practices, and values. Being culturally responsive requires a mindset that honors the needs of families and requires commitment to develop deep knowledge about the context of your community. This approach requires an authentic desire to learn about the perspectives of those who participate in your program.

⚙️ What Works Best: Using Culturally and Linguistically Responsive Teaching

Culturally and linguistically responsive teaching is an approach to preparation, practice, and mindset that ensures staff can respond to the needs of diverse families and help children of color be successful in the learning environment (Ladson-Billings 1995). It means teachers must "be competent in the ability to see cultural diversity as an asset and use cultural knowledge to develop the curriculum" (Djonko-Moor and Traum 2015). Modica, Ajmera, and Dunning (2010) note that without intentional review of family and teaching practices, programs may undermine culture and alienate children by threatening their sense of belonging. Therefore, culturally and linguistically responsive practice requires understanding the dynamics of bias and assurance that all practices honor and build on the strengths and resources of children and their families.

In its document "Quality Benchmark for Cultural Competence Project" (2009), NAEYC provides support for cultural competence in early childhood programs through staff acceptance of home languages, respect for home cultures, and the promotion of the active involvement of families. The quality benchmarks for cultural competence include a focus on the work of the program leader in fostering sensitivity among staff and leading ongoing training. This requirement includes "implementing a family-involvement awareness, orientation, and training program to ensure that all families know how to participate in the program and [that] all program staff know how to involve families in culturally sensitive ways."

While some situations you may encounter require simple respect and sensitivity, other circumstances will require deep humility and openness to learning and growing. As you make cultural responsiveness a priority, families will be your most important source of information. You can ask directly for feedback about their experiences, events, and needs. "Do you feel welcome here? What else can we do to support your family? Is there anything else you want to tell us? Are there any barriers that make you feel uncomfortable? Are there any experiences that make you feel comfortable?" Listen carefully to the responses.

This open communication will be the most important ingredient to your success. For example, what will you do when a child is from a religious background that does not celebrate birthdays and your program does? You will need to ask the family whether they are comfortable with alternative activities. What else would they like their child to do during this time? How would they like you to talk about the situation with him? How will the family talk to the child about differences?

When a child has visible special needs, how does the family want you to address this with other children? For example, one program provided dolls that represented differing physical special needs. Teachers used these to foster conversation during play and used teachable moments to encourage open conversations about children's strengths and differences. The mothers of two children who had mobility needs came to read books and answer questions for children. This was a positive learning experience for everyone.

The Whole Leadership Framework can guide your reflection and evaluation of your practices. What part of teaching and family engagement has been effective in involving families? Are there any barriers that may hinder open communication? How can you hire and train staff more effectively to understand the needs of your families? In what advocacy work can you best speak on behalf of the families you serve? What ways can you help your program as a whole become more sensitive and reflective in your practice? These questions can guide your growth as a program leader and be used to foster greater awareness and commitment among your staff.

⬚ Take-Away Strategies: Practicing Culturally Responsive Practice in Practical Ways

The following are practical ways your program can become more responsive to the needs of families in your program and community:

- Hire staff from the community you serve and who share the same race and cultural background as your families. Culturally matching role models are part of congruent and secure care for children.
- Get to know, mentor, and be mentored by program leaders from cultural backgrounds other than your own. Regular dialog about cultural responsiveness in leadership practices is important for ongoing accountability and growth.
- Evaluate your program's menu planning to be sure that you include food choices children enjoy at home.
- Reassess all classroom settings regularly to be sure they reflect the cultural frameworks of families, including music, stories, displays, and props. Children should see themselves reflected in stories not only in the illustrations but also in the typical experiences of the characters' lives.
- Evaluate the shared areas of your program setting to be sure they reflect cultural artifacts of families and the community.

- Make sure that your parent council or parent board is reflective of the diversity of the families in your community and that meetings are translated for non-English speakers.
- Be sure that family-support staff are from the community and have the same cultural background as families.
- Plan family events in the program or community that are of particular interest of the families and that are culturally respectful. For example, families may not feel comfortable attending an event alone but would like to participate in group events, such as the children's museum or library.
- Provide training to staff on diversity and anti-bias practices. Help staff to see and overcome their own biases by bringing in professional-development experts to facilitate training and reflection. Make sure this is an annual practice.
- Evaluate the language used in your program to be sure it is people centered and that all communication, messages, and goals are strength based and inclusive.

Supporting Dual Language Learners

Kaliyah and Amayah work diligently on a puzzle with Shea. Teacher Simone asks, "Can you find the missing puzzle piece? *¿Es el camión verde?* Is it the green truck?"

Kaliyah shrieks, "It's here!"

Simone smiles and says, "You found the green truck. Amayah, now you can work on the top section." She points to the top of the puzzle.

Shea says, "Almost done."

Simone replies, "You have all worked hard to find all the pieces."

Simone encourages the children as they switch between languages during play. In this classroom, almost half the families speak Spanish at home. Director John assists staff in finding additional resources, such as bilingual books, posters, and music recordings. He budgets for updates to multicultural materials and props for dramatic play. Staff invite families to provide feedback and support. Together, they create a setting that fosters success for dual language learners.

In early childhood, many children are learning English at the same time they are acquiring a second language. For children under age eight, 32 percent in the United States have at least one parent who speaks a language other than English at home (Park et al. 2017). Staff must learn about first- and second-language acquisition and know what is needed to foster increasing competence in both languages.

A welcoming setting for dual language learners offers more than labeled materials or songs in multiple languages. It views children and families with linguistic differences as contributing important strengths and resources to a program. Each family brings a unique set of linguistic and cultural experiences, as well as preferences for language use that teachers can use to build on and strengthen learning (Baker 2019; Gillanders, Castro, and Franco 2014). Staff must gain insight into the ways that children best learn and must understand how culture and language experiences in the home, school, and community influence and support development.

The Whole Leadership Framework can assist you in addressing the needs of dual language learners through pedagogical and administrative leadership functions, as you set goals and guide program direction. You will act as an ambassador for the needs of children and families as you collaborate with organizations outside of your program. Your leadership and involvement within and outside of the program will help you create a strong framework of responsiveness that meets the specific linguistic needs of families and the community.

Facilitating communication with and among families is a critical function of program leadership. The following strategies can help you increase effectiveness in supporting dual language learners and their families.

- Provide the program handbook and resources in English and in families' home languages.
- Ask families for feedback about communication. What else would they like to know? What are the best formats, such as phone messages, texts, written notes, email, or personal conversation, to receive information? What else can you include in program communication, priorities, and activities?
- Secure a translator and/or cultural broker to be present at meetings as needed to assist with communication needs.
- Partner with local community colleges, universities, or agencies to secure classroom volunteers to read to children in home languages and to translate and label books and materials. Preservice teacher-preparation programs often seek programs that can partner to provide participation experiences for students.
- Invite families to share stories, songs, books, and artifacts for the classroom and to read in home languages.
- Connect families with other families within your program for mentoring and/or mutual support. A biweekly coffee event works well to host these connections.
- Offer family events that focus on dual language acquisition and literacy.
- Connect with organizations in your community, such as community centers, park districts, and libraries, that provide resources in families' home languages.
- Facilitate ongoing professional development for staff that offers information and strategies to build competence in communicating with and supporting families.

The following resources offer a wealth of information and strategies to address the needs of dual language learners and their families.

- The WIDA *Early Years Guiding Principles of Language Development* provides information for program leaders and teachers. WIDA resources include *Early English Language Development Standards*, WIDA CAN DO Descriptors, and family engagement resources and strategies. In addition, staff can find guiding principles to support their work with children and their families. See: https://wida.wisc.edu/teach/early/elds

- The U.S. Department of Health and Human Services Administration for Children and Families offers a dual language learners toolkit: https://www.acf.hhs.gov/ecd/dual-language-learners

- The Frank Porter Graham Child Development Institute offers current research reports and briefs about dual language learning and teaching: https://cecerdll.fpg.unc.edu/document-library

- The U.S. Department of Education provides a report on dual language learners in the early years: https://www.ed.gov/early-learning/resources

- The Sheltered Instruction Observation Protocol (SIOP) website offers a research-based framework, professional development supports and handouts, and information about lesson plans and activities: http://www.cal.org/siop/resources

Understanding Trauma-Informed Teaching

Natalie arrives without an extra change of clothing. Her grandmother says, "I am just watching Natalie today. I don't know who will bring her tomorrow."

Director Sam asks, "Do you know when Natalie's mother will be back?"

The grandmother replies, "No. I am taking Natalie to her aunt's house today."

Sam responds kindly, "We have extra clothing and diapers for Natalie. We will talk with you again on Friday morning when you come back."

Increasingly, early childhood professionals see the consequences of stress and trauma in young children and their families. When child-care staff are supportive and provide safe and high-quality care, families are more able to be resilient. However, when basic needs are not met or multiple stress factors are present over time, more serious impacts occur. When the stress response is "extreme, long-lasting, and buffering relationships are unavailable to the child, the result can be toxic stress, leading to damaged, weakened bodily systems and brain architecture, with lifelong repercussions" (National Scientific Council on the Developing Child 2005/2014). For these reasons, understanding and promoting trauma-informed teaching is a priority for early childhood programs.

Unfortunately, trauma occurs frequently. According to an April 27, 2017 report from Child Trends, more than one quarter of confirmed cases of child abuse and neglect occur for children under age three. Nearly half of all children experience one or more types of trauma (Bartlett et al. 2017). The authors note that studies indicate up to 70 percent of children experience three or more a highly stressful or traumatic events by the time they are six years old. The National Center for Children in Poverty Young Child Risk Calculator shows that with each additional stress factor, children are increasingly vulnerable to detrimental effects (2018). Early childhood programs have a responsibility to connect families with early screening and to ensure they receive needed services.

Stress results from family or neighborhood violence; physical, emotional, or sexual abuse; the deaths or medical challenges of family members; addiction or incarceration in the family; and other environmental health risks (Dinehart et al. 2013). Interruption of reliable resources and family trauma during the prenatal period and early childhood years can be toxic, especially when appropriate intervention is unavailable (DeSocio 2015). Toxic stress compromises children's hormonal systems and brain and regulatory systems with detrimental effects on learning and development (Lipina 2016; National Scientific Council on the Developing Child 2010). Intervening early with education, support, and stress mediation in early childhood programs is essential.

Your program is an important part of coordinated trauma-informed systems. The National Child Traumatic Stress Network website (2018) states that trauma-informed systems "recognize and respond to the impact of traumatic stress on those who have contact with the system, including children, caregivers, and services providers. They act in collaboration with all who are involved with the child, using the best available science to maximize physical and psychological safety, facilitate the recovery of the child and family, and support their ability to thrive." Early childhood programs may be the first point of entry that can connect high-risk families with community mental-health consultation resources (Mortensen and Barnett 2016). In addition, they can facilitate responsive, high-quality care with caring staff who act as a protective buffer and help children thrive.

⚙ What Works Best: Connecting Stress and Program Quality

Stress and trauma can be visible or invisible. The effects can be seen at times in young children's behavior as stress and trauma impact memory, attention, and learning (McCrory et al. 2010). Stress also impacts staff and may result in inconsistent quality of care or a high degree of absenteeism. These factors affect the overall quality of teachers' relationships with children and families (Friedman-Krauss 2014; Whitaker et al. 2015). The ability of teachers to manage challenges in the classroom is compromised (Sparks 2017). Stress affects overall job performance and increases staff turnover (Phillips et al. 2016). Program leaders must directly address individual staff needs to create an integrated and ongoing culture of support.

Children who experience stress depend on consistent caregivers who are attuned to their needs and foster competence in all areas of development (Holmes et al. 2015). When recovering from short-term stress and when managing chronic stress over time, children depend on supportive, emotionally responsive relationships with adults who intervene with consistent modeling and care (Wright and Ryan 2014). Teachers must be emotionally responsive to provide needed support for classroom success (Hatfield et al. 2013).

By working with families and providing safe environments, early childhood programs can foster children's resilience and self-efficacy (Sciaraffa et al. 2018). Program leaders can act as advocates to foster awareness and understanding of the consequences of stress on brain development. They can collaborate with others in the community to strengthen and integrate all systems that support children and families' health and well-being.

🖼 Take-Away Strategies: Strengthening Family Resilience

Consider the aspects of whole leadership that touch the lives of families on a daily basis. Information in the program handbook, family-engagement events, and strategic planning for your program can place a priority on trauma-informed teaching and care. You can be responsive to the specific needs of families and children in your program as you evaluate existing supports and set goals to better address these needs. Ask for input from staff and families about the kinds of supports that will be helpful in your setting. Strategies to increase effectiveness include the following:

- Connecting families to early screening and community mental-health support services
- Providing information to families on the importance of rest, nutrition, and predictability in routines and schedules
- Featuring monthly connections to community, faith-based, and nonprofit resources that can provide direct support and assistance to staff and families
- Sharing positive guidance and calming strategies with families to strengthen children's skills, ensure consistent expectations, and provide scaffolding for success

- Creating a quiet and cozy space in each classroom where children can have time alone
- Giving book lists to families and sharing picture books that focus on emotional competence and problem-solving skills
- Communicating about daily routines and schedules with families and asking for feedback about differences between home and school, with the goal of providing congruent experiences
- Offering a library of books and resources families can check out that provide support for health and wellness, mental health, parenting skills, and positive guidance approaches
- Inviting health professionals and community child-development experts to address stress and stress mediation with your staff and parents
- Offering a space for families to meet together to talk with or mentor other families
- Joining a community-collaboration group to address and advocate for the safety, health, and education resources needed for families in your community

As you prioritize stress mediation in your program, invite staff to talk about the ways they see and experience stress personally. Ask them to share the ways they view stress in their children and families. Place trauma-informed teaching on the staff meeting agenda. Provide resources for reading and review. Trauma-informed teaching approaches ensure that all program staff are purposeful about noticing the needs of staff and families and the consequences of stress and trauma. It means working together with all staff members to ensure the health and resilience of all who participate in your program.

Using Coordinated Models of Care

> Jackson's mother, Felicia, sings a silly song as she changes his diaper. Then she says, "I always give him something to hold while I change his diaper. He likes to hold a toy car best. It distracts him. Sometimes he sings the song with me, but most of the time, he just plays."
>
> Teacher Bolin watches and says, "It helps to watch you interact with Jackson. I will use the same approach and song with him."

For infants and toddlers, leaving the predictable setting of home routines, the sights, smells, and sounds of daily life, and the direct attention of a familiar family caregiver can be stressful. When staff work with families to coordinate care, they make sure that schedules, patterns of events, and approaches to routines and self-care are similar. This communicates a sense of safety and security to children.

To children, family is their identity and source of love and sustenance. The strengths of the family unit should be integrated with classroom activities and approaches so there is continuity between the home and group setting. This integrated approach to the nurturing and teaching of children is called a *coparenting model of care* or a *cocaring framework* (Lang et al. 2016). A coparenting model creates strong scaffolding for children's emotional security. It supports their ability to develop secure attachment relationships. An integrated approach to nurturing and teaching also helps families feel confident in the daily quality of care received by their children.

In the same way, continuity of care refers to the priority placed on the relationship between the caregiver or teacher and child. *Continuity of care* is defined by care provided by the same person over an extended period of time, ideally for the first three years of life (Longstreth et al. 2016). Cocaring and continuity-of-care models ensure that families and children get to know caregivers well. They place a priority on full participation and open communication. Staff and families together recognize the essential needs of all children and commit to secure relationships and predictable caregiving.

In responsive infant and toddler settings, a single caregiver is the primary responder to children. This adult establishes trust and connection and has intimate knowledge of each child. During the day, the patterns of care routines, such as rocking, playing, songs, books, and activities, reflect the kinds of experiences children have in their family settings. This mindset can guide staff as they talk with families to learn from them what works best for their child at home.

The ratio of child to family members at home encourages intimate awareness of a child's needs. In the same way, small caregiver-to-child ratios in group settings allow staff to know children well. Staff are physically close and emotionally attuned with children throughout the day. When a child is hungry, tired, or unable to reach a desired toy, the caregiver's response time, mannerisms, and way of responding should feel familiar and comforting to the child.

During diaper changes and toileting routines, the level of care, the language used, and the reassurance and support offered need to be consistent. During meals, the food tastes and smells should be similar to what children experience at home. While eating, the table talk and proximity of a responsive adult should feel like a family. There should be a strong emotional bond, filled with warm conversation, shared smiles and laughter, making mealtimes and snack times enjoyable and fulfilling. It is important to be sensitive to the daily experiences of young children and to understand the way they feel in response to the care, teaching, and nurturing they receive.

To be effective in communication with families, program staff must have a deep pedagogical knowledge of child development and be able to apply developmentally appropriate practice. This means that staff recognize there are typical and predictable ranges and sequences of developmental progress. Children grow at their own rates and in their own unique ways. In addition, development is *asynchronistic*, meaning that a child may be advanced in one area, such as in physical dexterity or language development, but may require support in another area, such as social development. Young children are inconsistent day to day and require patient, individual support; positive guidance; and encouragement (Masterson 2018). For these reasons, working closely with families to communicate about daily progress and needs is a critical part of coordinated care. Successful communication requires ongoing learning, reflection, patience, good humor, and empathy.

Coordinated care includes coordinating experiences within the program. This is called *horizontal continuity*, and includes children's direct experiences within and across a program (Institute of Medicine and National Research Council 2015). Similarly, *vertical continuity* includes the ways programs communicate, plan, and coordinate across larger systems that affect children's development. These elements of cohesive and integrated approaches can be seen in the Whole Leadership Framework, which encompasses all of the ways your leadership functions strengthen the effectiveness of your program and influence the lives of children and families.

O─x Legacy of Leadership: Learning to Listen

"The best thing I ever did was listen to families and keep an open door. I stayed accessible. When teachers allowed children to play outside, a father became upset because he felt the child was dirty when he came to pick her up. The mother felt this was a reflection of her parenting. Rather than defend the importance of active play, I heard her need. We devised a plan to make sure the child's face was clean and to change her clothes if needed before the father picked her up. Over time, our small actions of respect built a sense of trust with the family."

Take-Away Strategies: Coordinating Care

When childrearing approaches and values are shared between families and programs, there is a sense of familiarity; however, when children and families encounter new situations or families hold ideas about childrearing that conflict, an extra dose of patience, compassion, and respect are needed. Program leaders, staff, and families may have the best of intentions, but may not be sure how to alleviate barriers to understanding.

Staff will benefit from an ongoing open forum to talk with you and other staff members about the best ways to communicate with families. They can learn from each other as they reflect on their experiences and explore the ways culture, language, and family practices influence caregiving techniques and children's responses. They can explore their own upbringing and evaluate experiences that inform their personal and professional perspectives.

Staff sensitivity to families and children requires thoughtful reflection about gaps in training, about bias and personal emotions, and about the need for honest appraisal of the dynamics of interpersonal communication. The following questions can help you discuss issues with staff and become more proactive in communicating with families.

- As you talk with families, ask for feedback about communication and caregiving.
  - How do you feel about communication between you and your child's teacher?
  - What other information do you wish you had?
  - What else would you like to tell us?
  - What else would you like us to do for and with your child?
  - What caregiving routines would you like to talk about or do you have questions about?
- As you talk with staff, explore the perspective of children.
  - What do experiences in the classroom look and feel like to children?
  - How and why do children benefit from coordinated care?
  - How can you better coordinate care?
  - What positive experiences with family communication can be shared at staff meetings to benefit learning for all staff?
- Brainstorm additional people and resources that can provide information about the needs of families in your community.
  - What programs, events, and materials can help staff better support families?
  - How can families provide greater support and resources for other families?

Chapter 6 Study Guide: Assessing Family Engagement from a Whole Leadership Perspective

Building Bridges

When you practice something with children in your program that is practiced differently in a child's home, communication and patience will be needed. For example, when programs practice family-style meals, children are expected to serve themselves and stop when they feel full. In some families, hand feeding, allowing children walk around during meals, or making children finish all their food is customary. How do you communicate with families about practices that differ between home and program, such as family-style meals? Some program practices may be considered nonnegotiable, and others can be adapted to ensure consistency. Write several examples that demonstrate how staff in your program have adapted their practice to be consistent with what is practiced in the home environment.

_____

_____

_____

_____

_____

_____

In what ways can you learn about family practices to better serve the children in your care?

_____

_____

_____

_____

_____

_____

_____

_____

Embedding Family Engagement through Whole Leadership

How do you embed family engagement into your program practices? Check all that apply:

Practice	Yes	No
Potential families are given a reference list of past and current families, as well as a link to the program's website that contains family testimonials.	☐	☐
The family handbook includes a section on family engagement, demonstrating how families are considered partners and how family engagement is valued	☐	☐
Photos of family members engaging with children are displayed throughout the program.	☐	☐
New families are introduced to current families and paired to support one another.	☐	☐
Lesson plans include a space and questions to link content to children's experience in family life.	☐	☐
Each family receives a home visit, which includes collecting information about the unique aspects of the family and the ways home life and program experiences can be seamless.	☐	☐
After the child's first week of enrollment, there is a "touch base" phone call to find out how the transition is working and to identify adjustments that can be made to acclimate the child to the program.	☐	☐
Teaching team meetings include a standing agenda item for updates about families.	☐	☐
Each child has a notebook in her cubby that travels back and forth between home and program so families and teachers are kept informed about the daily happenings in the child's life.	☐	☐
Family conferences happen at least twice a year and are used to provide a thorough explanation of children's learning and development, with ideas for ways families can support learning and development during daily routines at home.	☐	☐
Supervisors of teachers include family partnerships as a criterion they address during supervision meetings.	☐	☐
Job descriptions include criteria on family engagement, and staff are evaluated on these criteria.	☐	☐
Staff read books related to family engagement and participate in book-club discussions.	☐	☐
When staff read books or articles or attend workshops on family engagement, a supervisor follows up on this topic during reflective-supervision meetings.	☐	☐
Staff who attend training complete a form that includes space to capture insights learned and methods for implementation.	☐	☐
Teachers are expected to implement a practice learned from reading or training and to discuss the outcomes with their supervisor and/or colleagues.	☐	☐
Once staff have an opportunity to practice, reflect, implement, and tweak what they have learned during a training, they are encouraged to present the new practice, as well as lessons learned, at a meeting with their colleagues.	☐	☐
The program has a video clip that highlights family engagement practices.	☐	☐

Adapted from Bella, Jill. 2016. *A Critical Intersection: Administrative and Pedagogical Leadership.* Wheeling, IL: McCormick Center for Early Childhood Leadership. Used with permission.

Advancing Administrative Leadership

In this chapter, we explore the elements of administrative leadership, including core functions, tools, and effect on the health and vitality of your organization. Chapter 8 presents the tools for administrative leadership and how these contribute to the effectiveness of your organization.

Administrative Leadership Core	Tools for Administrative Leadership	Impact on Organizational Health and Vitality
Operational leadership: ensuring adequate equipment and space, guiding the development and management of budgets, fostering a positive workplace, and hiring and supporting staff	• Ability to develop talent • Systems thinking • Financial and legal knowledge and skills • Awareness of organizational climate	• Qualified, consistent staff • Collaborative teams • Organizational supports for teaching in place • Positive organizational climate
Strategic leadership: goal setting and guiding future program direction	• Ability to interpret data and plan strategically • Public-relations and marketing expertise • Entrepreneurial focus	• Stable organization that adapts to change and grows to meet needs • Embedded norms of continuous quality improvement
Advocacy leadership: acting as an ambassador for the needs of children, families, and programs	• Communication skills • Knowledge of public policies affecting children and families • Affiliation with professional organizations	• Proactive rather than reactive to changes in external environment • Empower staff and families to advocate for their needs
Community leadership: collaborating with organizations on behalf of the children and families served	• Knowledge of early childhood systems (health, family support, education) • Ability to collaborate across systems (health, family support, education)	• Strong relationships with local community stakeholders • Coordinated services for children and families

107

Ensuring Optimal Operational Leadership

Leila is the director of a Reggio-inspired early childhood program located in a large metropolitan area. She tells a visiting board member from her organization, "I am really excited about the art studio that the teaching staff developed for the children. It's lovely to look at and filled with materials to entice children to explore and create. I love the sensory elements—small stones the children collected at the lakefront that are attached to the walls in a meandering design just at the right height for small hands to touch. This project grew out of a staff meeting last year. I asked everyone to reflect on their dreams for the children in their classes and how our center might help those dreams come true. One idea emerged from this exercise that excited everyone—to create a special space dedicated to children's artistic expression. The educators got busy planning and renovating an underutilized store room. I told them what financial resources were available, offered my help if they needed it, and turned the project over to them. Collectively the teaching staff, interested families, and even some of the children, made all the decisions. I see teaching and learning come alive every day in our new art studio."

What Leila describes is a program with a healthy organizational climate—a true learning organization. The staff demonstrate authentic teamwork built on collegiality and reciprocal trust. In a healthy organizational climate, teachers and other staff feel comfortable sharing their ideas. They collaborate to solve problems. They share in leadership decisions. They know that their supervisor will support them and help them learn from any mistakes made as they try something new.

Leila realizes that meaningful interactions such as brainstorming, analysis of ideas, and collaborative decision making during staff meetings only happen when there is positive, appreciative, and open communication. She knows how to instill norms of collaboration and ensure commitment to the organization's mission of high-quality early care and education. Leila demonstrates supervisor support by distributing leadership to staff with a high level of competence and interest to see the art studio project through to completion. She mentors her staff as well as other directors in the community to encourage professional growth.

Tessa is a newly minted director, recently promoted from the position of a pre-K lead teacher at Leila's center. Tessa was recognized as an outstanding teacher and was sure that her expertise would transfer to her new role. However, she has encountered challenges and contacts Leila, who is willing to mentor her in her new leadership role.

Tessa shares with Leila, "Last week I held my first staff meeting and I knew I was in trouble. I asked staff for items to be put on the agenda and received no requests. No problem—I had plenty of topics to address. I wasn't, however, prepared for the radio silence from staff at the meeting. One example had to do with enhancing outdoor play. I shared my observation that teachers are talking to each other in the outdoor play area, acting as safety monitors rather than interacting with children. I asked what might improve the quality of the children's outdoor play. There was no response. I asked, 'Do we need to purchase new materials? Bring paint or chalk outdoors? How do the teaching teams plan for outdoor curriculum?' Their nonverbal communication, with no one meeting my eyes, told me they were afraid to speak up. I felt the chill in the room even though it was summer."

Leila tells Tessa about resources to ensure a positive organizational climate in her program, and Tessa responds immediately. She collects data from her staff using the Early Childhood Work Environment Survey (ECWES). Staff members fill out a brief and confidential survey related to the ten dimensions of organizational climate (see the chart on page 110). The results are tallied and a work environment profile is generated. Tessa distributes the profile in advance of a staff meeting. At the meeting, they use the results of the ECWES to develop a plan of action. The three dimensions that staff perceive as lowest at the program become the three focus areas for a plan to improve the organizational climate.

⚙️ What Works Best: Retaining Quality Staff

Research over the past decade on early childhood program quality has found a significant positive relationship between the quality of administrative practices and the quality of the children's learning environment in center-based programs (Dennis and O'Connor 2013; Lower and Cassidy 2007; McCormick Center for Early Childhood Leadership 2010; Kagan et al. 2008). Research also suggests that one aspect of administrative practice—fostering a positive work environment—can help reduce staff turnover (Whitebook et al. 2014).

The data on turnover tells an interesting story. Nationally, about 30 percent of center teaching staff leave each year (Porter 2012). However, this average turnover rate masks difference among centers and among the different roles of teaching staff. Illinois data from 2017 show a two-year turnover rate of 39 percent for assistant teachers and 31 percent for teachers (Whitehead et al. 2016). The turnover rate for all teaching positions was reduced to 17 percent when staff received a wage supplement through the state-funded Great START program. This program provides a graduated wage supplement for staff who have higher qualifications (education and credentials) than the minimum requirements as defined in licensing standards. This research suggests that program leaders who support the professional development of their staff are more likely to retain them.

In their book *A Great Place to Work: Creating a Healthy Organizational Climate*, authors Paula Jorde Bloom, Ann Hentschel, and Jill Bella assert that "taking steps to improve your center's organizational climate is an effective way to increase staff morale, enhance program quality, and perhaps even reduce teacher turnover . . . In a field plagued with high turnover, it makes good sense to direct our attention toward establishing work environments that foster high levels of commitment."

In addition to supporting professional development through education and credential attainment for staff, creating job-embedded learning teams can also positively affect teacher retention. In a study conducted in the Chicago Public Schools, researchers found that the quality of the work environment predicted whether teachers remained in their schools. A critical factor was the teachers' perceptions of whether or not their teams were collaborative (Allensworth et al. 2009).

Building trust and implementing change takes time. Tessa knows that the high turnover rate of teachers in her program has resulted in the teaching teams being unable to meet, reflect on their practice, and plan curriculum together. One important change Tessa wants to make moving forward is to protect time for the teaching teams to learn from each other by working collaboratively on curriculum. Tessa knows she can't wave a magic wand to make this happen. She needs to allocate more resources—staff, time, and money—to ensure the organizational supports are there for effective teaching and adequate coverage in the classrooms. Tessa realizes she needs additional financial-management skills to make this goal a reality.

Leila, her mentor, shares her go-to resources and websites about financial planning and change management. Tessa decides to enroll in an online course designed to develop early childhood business acumen. By enrolling in this course, Tessa anticipates she will gain the administrative competencies she needs to take charge of change. She also wants to model for the center staff her commitment to continuous professional development.

Ten Dimensions of Organizational Climate

Dimension	Definition
Collegiality	The extent to which staff are friendly, supportive, and trusting of one another; the peer cohesion and esprit de corps of the group
Professional growth	The availability of opportunities to increase professional competence and the degree of emphasis placed on staff's professional growth
Supervisor support	The degree of facilitative leadership providing encouragement, support, and clear expectations
Clarity	The extent to which policies, procedures, and responsibilities are clearly defined and communicated
Reward system	The degree of fairness and equity in the distribution of pay, fringe benefits, and opportunities for advancement
Decision making	The degree of autonomy given to staff and the extent to which they are involved in making center-wide decisions
Goal consensus	The extent to which staff agree on the philosophy, goals, and educational objectives of the center
Task orientation	The emphasis placed on organizational effectiveness and efficiency, including productive meetings, program outcomes, and accountability
Physical setting	The extent to which the spatial arrangement of the center helps or hinders staff in carrying out their responsibilities; the availability of supplies and materials
Innovativeness	The extent to which the center adapts to change and encourages staff to find creative ways to solve problems

From Bloom, Paula Jorde. 2016. *Measuring Work Attitudes in the Early Childhood Setting: Technical Manual for the Early Childhood Job Satisfaction Survey and Early Childhood Work Environment Survey.* 3rd ed. Wheeling, IL: National Louis University, McCormick Center for Early Childhood Leadership. Reprinted with permission.

Inspiring Strategic Leadership through Goal Setting

Lakeshia is the executive director of a suburban nonprofit child-development center serving approximately fifty preschool children and fifty school-age children. She talks with a group of directors in her town. "Two years ago my program was half this size and served only preschoolers. I wanted a high-quality program, but this was a struggle when the only administrator was me. I was covering in the classrooms when teachers were absent, hiring and supervising staff, managing payroll and expenses, collecting tuition, and responding to a governing board. I was working fifty to sixty hours a week—a recipe for burnout. I saw other programs closing their doors.

"Today, I have an assistant director, Gio, who helps me with both leadership and management functions. We work closely with the educators on improving their teaching practices. I support the preschool team, and Gio supports the school-age team. We've joined a shared services alliance to manage many of the business tasks. We've outsourced enrollment, tuition collection, payroll, and expense management. I've even achieved more of a work-life balance. We see a big impact in our ability to deliver a consistent and high-quality program."

Lakeshia worked with the governing board, which includes current and former families enrolled in the center, to develop a two-year strategic plan to achieve significant growth and stability. She first conducted a needs assessment, surveying families about their child-care needs. Many families indicated a desire for a school-age program that would align with the mission, vision, and values of their preschool program. The preschool teaching staff were excited about this expansion possibility and the idea of extending their relationships with children and families for an additional three years. Next, Lakeshia conducted a market analysis. The center is well-situated in a neighborhood with three nearby elementary schools. There is little competition within the community for school-age programming with an early childhood focus. The board developed an endowment-fund strategy while Lakeshia wrote grants for facility improvements. Ultimately, all of these strategies were successful.

⚙️ What Works Best: Making Connections between Administrative and Pedagogical Leadership

The following cooking metaphor is one way for you to think about the interdependence of administrative and pedagogical leadership in your programs. Early childhood educators need consistent feedback on their practice and ongoing support for teaching excellence. Instructional leadership is indeed that "secret sauce." Sometimes, it may seem that you are preparing a meal but only paying attention to the sauce. Overseeing the teaching functions of your program often consumes a great deal of your time.

Administrative leadership is needed to ensure that the organizational structures and processes are in place to support staff as they nurture the development and learning of young children and build partnerships with families. You can think of administrative leadership as the entrée needing pedagogical leadership, the sauce, to be complete.

Administrative leadership is interdependent with pedagogical leadership. These domains work together as part of continuous quality improvement (CQI) efforts. CQI is both a philosophy and a sequence of intentional practices used to improve administrative as well as teaching practices within early childhood programs. In a report for BUILD, a collaboration for strategic early childhood systems-building, author Billie Young writes, "CQI is optimally seated in an organizational culture that has a common vision, shared values and beliefs, and a commitment to ongoing quality improvement. CQI is reflective, cyclical, and data-driven. It is proactive, not reactive. It goes beyond merely meeting externally applied standards and moves the lever for change internally. Participants control the process themselves, through continuous learning and a dedication to getting better at getting better" (Young 2017).

Strategic leadership involves members of a team in a collaborative, reflective cycle—using a Plan, Do, Study, Act strategy—and includes the following elements of a program-improvement structure and process:

- Identifying and analyzing strengths and weaknesses based on data
- Establishing a plan with benchmarks, timelines, assigned tasks, and responsibilities to improve
- Testing and implementing solutions; evaluating the results and revising the plan as needed (Bloom 2015; Douglass 2017).

In "Taking Charge of Change: A Twenty-Year Review of Empowering Early Childhood Administrators through Leadership Training," the authors offer three take-away lessons to be learned about the program-improvement process:

- Personal change typically precedes organizational change.
- Organizational change is most successful and lasting when it is implemented in small, incremental steps.
- Systemic change is slow.

(Talan et al. 2014; Bloom et al. 2013)

Program leaders may feel compelled to make big changes in their programs. State quality rating and improvement may inadvertently contribute to this pressurized state for the administrative and teaching staff in early learning settings. However, research demonstrates that a better way to achieve lasting change is by adopting the approach of *kaizen*, a Japanese term that translates as "good change." Author Robert Maurer (2013) explains: "When you need to make a change, there are two basic strategies you can use: innovation and *kaizen*. Innovation calls for a radical, immediate rethink of the status quo. *Kaizen*, on the other hand, asks for nothing other than small, doable steps toward improvement."

O—🗝 Legacy of Leadership: Taking Charge of Change©

Bettye has been a teacher and family educator and is now a program administrator at a community-based early learning center. Through her participation in the Taking Charge of Change (TCC) leadership academy, she developed a year-long program-improvement plan. She chose her goals using the results of administering the ECWES with all center staff. Bettye focused on improving the organizational climate by building trust, enhancing collaboration, and improving collegiality. To achieve these objectives, she looked for more opportunities to show appreciation to staff; worked on mission, vision, and values with staff members, families, and the board; practiced expressing feelings in a safe, nonjudgmental way; engaged staff in the program planning process; provided anti-bias training; empowered staff to make decisions that affect their work; and, finally, had fun with her team.

Bettye offers this reflection: "At a staff meeting, I shared the story I learned at TCC of the boy who walks along the shore throwing beached starfish back into the sea. His father asks why he bothers when there are so many starfish left stranded on the beach. The boy responds that it matters to the starfish that are saved. I want my staff to know that small things matter. And each one of them is valued for their contribution."

Understanding Advocacy Leadership as Part of Early Childhood Systems

Sonia, the director of an early learning program located in a public school that serves young dual language learners, shares her story at a conference. "First, I took an equity issue—the need for full-day, full-year programming—to the school administration. I communicated with the preschool and kindergarten teachers in the district to enlist their support. Then I learned that there are local advocacy organizations that could provide national data and communications support. We also worked with the local parent teacher association and the chamber of commerce to advance our cause. Families and the business community became strong allies. We had close to one hundred people in attendance at the next school-board meeting. I was one of the speakers even though I am extremely introverted. I was nervous to speak up and challenge the existing policy. I was one of many voices, but as the director of the program, I felt it made a difference. Next year, our district will begin a full-day early learning program to meet the needs of our growing immigrant population."

Advocacy leadership is acting on behalf of children, families, staff, and programs. It means speaking up and speaking out for what is needed, based on your knowledge of child development and family systems, experience in early care and education, and commitment to social justice. Advocacy leadership and community leadership are important aspects of strategic leadership. While strategic leadership is internally focused on personal and organizational development, advocacy leadership and community leadership are externally focused on making systemic changes.

Why is advocacy leadership a core function of administrative leadership within the Whole Leadership Framework? Your organization is an open social system comprised of interconnected parts: external environment, people, structure, processes, culture, and outcomes. Early care and education programs do not exist in an impermeable bubble. Each early childhood center sits within a larger context of organizations in the local community as well as state and national organizations. Stakeholders include Head Start and universal pre-K programs, child care resource and referral agencies, and community colleges and universities.

The external environment exerts a strong influence on your early childhood program in terms of required health and safety regulations, such as child-care licensing standards or school codes, and enhanced quality standards associated with national accreditation, Head Start, and state QRIS. Effective program leaders see their programs as open systems, recognizing their dependence on the broader environment. See the components of a system in the diagram below.

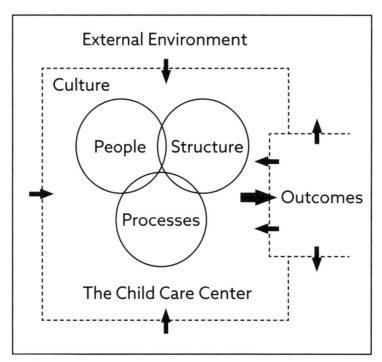

Source: Bloom, Paula Jorde. 2015. *Blueprint for Action: Leading Your Team in Continuous Quality Improvement.* 3rd ed. Lake Forest, IL: New Horizons.

⚙ What Works Best: Being Forward Thinking and Future Oriented

In their seminal book *Leadership in Early Care and Education*, editors Kagan and Bowman (1997) include a chapter on advocacy leadership written by Helen Blank. She identifies the competencies associated with advocacy leadership:

- Having a vision, planning for the long term, and moving beyond the press of everyday responsibilities
- Collaborating with colleagues
- Reaching out and working with people who are not familiar colleagues
- Looking for strategic opportunities
- Making strategic use of data
- Developing new approaches to reach the public and policymakers
- Making tough decisions that may involve personal risk
- Hanging tough, being relentless, and continually developing new approaches to advance your issue
- Knowing how and when to compromise
- Inspiring and supporting new leaders

Two decades later, these competencies are still needed by early childhood advocates. Today's pressing issues, including racial equity and compensation parity, and strategic opportunities are different from those described by Blank in 1997, but the knowledge, skills, and dispositions remain the same. For more information, see the Institute of Medicine and National Research Council's report *Transforming the Workforce for Children Birth through Age 8: A Unifying Foundation* and NAEYC's Power to the Profession initiative.

⚷ Legacy of Leadership: Participating in State Advocacy

Moriah is the director of a child-development center that has served her community for more than seventy-five years. Each year, she participates in the annual Child Care Lobby Day organized by several statewide early childhood organizations. She explains to her staff, "I wanted to invite our program graduates, who are now in middle school, to participate in Lobby Day as a strategic opportunity to develop new early childhood leaders and get the attention of legislators. I reached out to the families to share my idea. I provided a description of the Child Care Lobby Day, including its bipartisan approach to state advocacy for families, to share with their respective schools. I stressed the age-appropriate field experience in civics and leadership development. The end result is that Jimi, Xiaoli, and Morgan went with us to the state capitol, collaborated with child-care advocates from across the state, and spoke to their legislators about the impact our early childhood program has had on their enthusiasm for learning. I believe a new generation of advocates was launched."

Building Advocacy Leadership for Collective Impact

> Sam is the early childhood director of a Montessori school serving children from infancy through the primary grades. He wants to encourage his staff to participate in a community-health initiative for children that works in collaboration with the children's hospital. "Let's work together to address screen time, healthy nutrition, and exercise. We can see these needs in our program. What ways can we address this? Would you like to participate in the community walk/run as a beginning step?"

After a lively discussion of the ideas, staff agree to participate in the walk/run. Sam offers to help a volunteer group of staff plan. Some review literature on child obesity; some meet with representatives from the health department, park district, elementary school district, and local early learning collaboration. They hold a follow-up meeting with the entire staff. Sam is pleased with the collective leadership demonstrated resulting in several creative strategies. Their program, in collaboration with many of the community organizations with which they met, agree to an action plan for a Screen-Free Week in their community. The participating community organizations, businesses, and schools agree to offer and promote free, active, and fun activities for the whole family.

What Works Best: Strengthening Community Partnerships

Community collaboration is critical to advancing a high-quality care and education agenda. One person, or even one organization, cannot make significant change given the complexity of the cross-sector early care and education system. Community leadership is closely related to two other leadership concepts: collective leadership and collective impact (O'Neill and Brinkerhoff 2017; Kania and Kramer 2011; W. K. Kellogg Foundation 2007). Collective leadership is needed to address the complex problems faced by young children, their families, and the communities in which they live.

Dwayne Crompton, in Kagan and Bowman's book *Leadership in Early Care and Education* (1997), writes about community leadership as being out in the community educating others in a way that mobilizes action. He stresses the important function of the community leader to serve as an early care and education expert, communicating a compelling story that secures both public funding and private investment. "A leader who can make meaning, who can demonstrate how an idea or point of view coincides with the values of the majority, will find it much easier to win the support of the community."

Poverty, educational inequity, hunger, bias, and homelessness impede a significant number of children from developing optimally. No one organization or single strategy can give children what they need to succeed. Foundations have come to realize that funding a single approach, whether it is quality early care and education or affordable housing or a universal health-care initiative, is not going to move the needle forward on changing child outcomes. The results of countless evaluation studies suggest that entrenched social problems need collective leadership that leads to collective impact at the community level.

⚷ Legacy of Leadership: Influencing Change

Josie shares with her colleagues, "I received a scholarship to attend a national conference designed specifically for early childhood program leaders. I participated in a session on collective impact, which got me thinking about viewing my program's challenges with enrollment from a wide-angled, systems perspective. I connected with directors from all over the country and learned of community collaborations that were finding solutions through partnerships across sectors. When I returned home, I started making exploratory calls. There are still bumps in the road, but today the facilitation of the community collaboration is funded by local businesses. The collaboration has successfully written for an Early Head Start/Child Care Partnership grant. The local school district has indicated a willingness to consider a mixed-delivery model for the state-funded pre-K program. I don't need credit for these positive developments. I keep in mind a quote from the Chinese philosopher, Lao-Tzu: 'When the best leader's work is done, the people say we did it ourselves.'"

Moving beyond Leadership versus Management to Making a Difference

Biyu addresses her colleagues at a local early childhood collaboration meeting. "As a director, I need to have a strong grasp of my budget in order to plan effectively for professional-development needs. How can I make decisions about ordering resources for my staff if I don't know how much money we can spend? I have to manage the budget before I can offer the resources. Leadership and management are intertwined. I need a working knowledge of both sides, like two strands of DNA, fully integrated and dependent on the other."

Administrative leadership is often blended with the idea of management. To be clear, both leadership and management are critical to effective program administration. Leadership functions relate to the broad view of guiding an organization to clarify and affirm values, set goals, articulate a vision, and chart a course of action to achieve that vision. Management functions relate to the orchestration of tasks and the design and implementation of systems to carry out the organizational mission (Talan and Bloom 2011).

Another way to think about the difference between leadership and management is temporal. Where do you invest your time and thinking? Leadership is forward thinking and directed toward future growth and development. Management is about present thinking and directed toward achieving current goals and objectives. The successful program leader pays close attention to both.

You can think metaphorically about the program director as an orchestra conductor (Bloom 2000). A conductor must know the strengths of each orchestra member and balance the parts (string, percussion, and brass sections) to achieve the goal of a harmonious and inspired symphony performance. This is an example of *synergy*—a mutually beneficial collaboration of elements—whose whole is greater than the sum of the parts. The effect of the performance is immediate and discernable by the standing ovation and wet eyes of the audience. The orchestra conductor must also be forward thinking. He or she needs to help individual orchestra members grow their artistic sensibilities, select music for future performances, attract new audiences, and sustain the reputation of the orchestra as a whole.

You, as an administrative leader, are making a difference in the lives of children, families, and staff each day. You are that conductor—balancing the priorities of enrolling children and families; developing financial resources; hiring, supporting, and scheduling staff; ensuring consistent operations; planning effective meetings; working with your governing or advisory board; reviewing the strategic plan; and collaborating with other organizations in the community to best meet the needs of children, families, staff, and programs. As you juggle the many responsibilities of administrative leadership in real time, you must be both present- and future-oriented. Leadership versus management is therefore a false dichotomy. What matters is the potential to make a lasting impact in the lives of children and families today and those you will serve in the future.

O— Legacy of Leadership: Inspiring Passion for the Work

"Leadership is not about a title or a designation. It is about impact, influence, and inspiration. Impact involves getting results, influence is about spreading the passion you have for your work, and you have to inspire your team and customers."

—Robin S. Sharma, author and speaker

Chapter 7 Study Guide: Exploring Administrative Leadership

Administrative Leadership Skills

Administrative leadership has several core elements: operational, strategic, advocacy, and community. Rate your skill level in each, with 1 representing "not at all skilled" and 5 representing "completely skilled." Circle the answer that best represents your rating.

Core Element	Not at All Skilled	A Bit Skilled	Somewhat Skilled	Quite a Bit Skilled	Completely Skilled
Operational Leadership					
• Hiring and supporting staff	1	2	3	4	5
• Overseeing operations and budgets	1	2	3	4	5
• Fostering positive organizational climate	1	2	3	4	5
Strategic Leadership					
• Goal setting	1	2	3	4	5
• Guiding future program direction	1	2	3	4	5
Advocacy Leadership					
• Acting as an ambassador for the needs of children, families, staff, and programs	1	2	3	4	5
Community Leadership					
• Collaborating with organizations on behalf of the children and families served	1	2	3	4	5

Based on your ratings, what are your areas of strength?

_____

_____

_____

_____

_____

Which of these skills would you like to improve or develop further?

_____

_____

_____

_____

_____

What resources and action steps will help you develop your skills in these areas?

_____

_____

_____

_____

_____

Based on your ratings, what are areas for growth? What resources and action steps will help you develop your skills in these areas?

_____

_____

_____

_____

_____

Applying Tools for Effective Administrative Leadership

Tools for Administrative Leadership

- Ability to plan strategically
- Expertise in systems development
- Financial and legal knowledge and skills
- Awareness of organizational climate

- Public-relations and marketing expertise
- Entrepreneurial focus
- Ability to interpret data
- Public-engagement skills

The previous chapter described the four core areas of administrative leadership in detail. This chapter explores the tools for administrative leadership using director Charmaine's words and her organization's story to illuminate how these tools contribute to the effectiveness of her program. You may be pondering the differences between the core areas and the tools for application. The four core areas in chapter 7 outline the major functions of administrative leadership. They describe the "what" of effective administrative leadership.

The tools for application of effective administrative leadership provide the overarching competencies needed; they describe the "how." The tools allow you to be effective in administrative leadership to ensure organizational health. The research on the impact of administrative leadership shows why your work in this area matters.

Maximizing Operational Leadership

Charmaine is at her monthly meeting of the early childhood directors' network, which has focused for the past year on learning about and improving organizational climate and culture. Charmaine shares her success story. "Low morale and burnout were our biggest challenges. I assumed this was caused by low wages resulting in a high rate of teacher turnover. While I haven't been able to increase wages, the staff morale has definitely improved over the last six months. Our educators now have a salary scale that is transparent and equitable, and this has made a real difference. They see a pathway to greater opportunity within the organization as well as enhanced compensation. Another factor improving our work environment is all our efforts to create a culture of appreciation. I realize now the problem of morale wasn't all externally driven. I needed to work on myself. I now try to view each member of my staff through an appreciative lens—to see them as competent and capable—and then I think, how can I operationalize these values? The answer is working collaboratively with staff to ensure that our organization—through its structures and processes—supports them to be the best they can be."

Charmaine has a lot going for her. She participates regularly in a professional learning community, where she has peers with whom to share concerns and resources, problem solve, learn and grow professionally, and offer and receive support. This learning community is a safe place for Charmaine to talk openly about her challenges and successes as a program leader. The success story she shares with her peers demonstrates use of each of the tools of operational leadership.

Charmaine's story—a successful plan to increase staff morale—demonstrates attention to and modifications in all three components of a system: people, structure, and processes. First, she increased her knowledge by learning about appreciative inquiry as a management approach (Cooperrider and Srivastva 2017; Hammond 2013; Bloom, Hentschel, and Bella 2013). She addressed her own beliefs about the staff's capacity to be effective teachers and learners (the people component) before looking to change behavior in others. She worked to adopt an appreciative, strength-based approach to staff development and distributed her leadership when possible (Talan 2010; Spillane 2006; Bloom 2011).

In addition, Charmaine developed and discussed with staff a transparent and equitable salary scale (the structure component). She introduced a graduated salary scale based on role, education, specialized knowledge, and relevant experience. Making the salary scale accessible to all staff significantly improved their perceptions of the organization as having a fair and equitable reward system. Transparency in communications builds trust and promotes staff engagement (Jiang and Men 2017).

Finally, Charmaine made changes in how staff meetings would be facilitated and how center-wide decisions would be made (processes component). She made sure everyone had an opportunity to be heard at staff meetings by passing a "talking stick," and she made sure everyone had an opportunity to lead discussions by asking staff members to be responsible for agenda items. She shared her leadership authority by using a consensus-building approach to making center-wide, strategic decisions.

A child care organization is made up of people: children, families, volunteers, and staff; structures: legal requirements, policies, procedures, and physical environment; and processes: teaching, learning, communicating, leadership, and decision making. Each of these parts is interconnected—if you as the program leader make a change in just one of the parts, there will be some effect on the other parts of the system. If you want to make a long-lasting change, such as improving the climate of the work environment, you need to consider making change in each of these three interconnected parts. Good intentions to implement improvements that fail to achieve the desired outcomes are often the result of failing to think systematically.

⚙ What Works Best: Integrating Administrative Leadership Priorities

- **Integrating systems thinking:** Much has been written about systems theory and systems thinking over the past several decades (Brynteson 2006; Haines 2000; Senge 1990). Systems thinking is an important problem-solving skill for any organizational leader. It means taking a wide-angle view of your organization so that you see the whole as well as each of its parts. Systems thinking is also about seeing patterns and connecting the dots between cause and effect. You know the expression "You can't see the forest for the trees"? When you are adept at systems thinking, you are able to see both the forest and the trees at the same time.

- **Developing talent:** Charmaine's plan to boost staff morale was based on investing in her staff. She did more than create a salary scale. She also supported the teaching staff to attain formal education, specialized training, and credentials so they could advance on the salary scale. Her organization now offers a partial-tuition scholarship for college coursework. As part of the work environment improvement plan, Charmaine set up a mentoring system in which teacher leaders mentor other teachers struggling to balance work, family, and school responsibilities. The mentors even receive a small stipend. Charmaine is feeling hopeful about retaining more qualified teachers based on these investments because, with increased professional qualifications, many will qualify for the state's wage supplement program to retain a qualified early care and education workforce.

- **Applying financial and legal knowledge:** Charmaine holds her state's director credential requiring demonstrated competencies in financial management. She knew that her current budget couldn't stretch to increase wages across the board. The families in her program are of mixed incomes, but even the families who pay the full cost of tuition could not afford to pay more. The innovations introduced as part of her plan—paid mentors, partial scholarships, release time for staff to attend classes—came with a cost. The cost of paying teachers increased wages based on enhanced qualifications needed to be factored into financial planning for the future. Because Charmaine has financial knowledge and skills, she is able to reallocate current income, forecast a new source of revenue from an innovative fundraising event, decrease expenses, and demonstrate to the governing board that the organization can afford to implement these improvements.

- **Fostering a positive organizational climate:** As a savvy operational leader, Charmaine was keenly aware of the climate of her organization—using a weather metaphor, it was overcast with storms on the way. But unlike weather forecasts, you can't wait a day for the work environment to clear up. The first step is awareness: Are children happily engaged in play? Are teachers working well with each other? Are staff actively involved in meetings? Charmaine asked herself these questions and wasn't happy with her answers. Charmaine understood that, as the program leader, it is her responsibility to act on this awareness and foster a more positive organizational climate. Wearing her systems-thinking lenses, she was able to separate cause and effect, to distinguish the problem from the symptom. The tension she observed among teaching teams, the chronic absences of some staff, the negative nonverbal communication at staff meetings—these were all symptoms of a larger problem. To identify the root problem and determine the appropriate actions, Charmaine needed objective data.

Planning Strategically: Making the Most of Strategic Leadership

> Six months ago, Charmaine disseminated a work-environment survey to everyone on the staff, with instructions to fill it out and send it back electronically. She explained, "The information will be aggregated electronically and a work-environment profile generated. No responses will be connected to individuals; so rest assured you have complete confidentiality. Please be honest in your responses so that we can work together to improve our work environment. We will devote our next staff meeting to reviewing the profile and developing a plan. We will make time at subsequent staff meetings to update staff on the decisions made and to benchmark our progress. We will continue until collectively we say this is a great place to work."

Charmaine needs data to develop a solid plan to improve the work climate. She also realizes she can't fix the negative climate by herself. She will need the engagement—indeed, the leadership—of staff and families to ultimately ensure the success of the quality-improvement plan to boost staff morale and prevent teacher burnout. The success of Charmaine's efforts depends on using the tools of strategic leadership.

The three tools for strategic leadership are using data to plan strategically, developing expertise in public relations and marketing, and adopting an entrepreneurial focus. Together, these will strengthen your influence and improve outcomes.

- **Using data to plan strategically:** To achieve a goal, you need a plan of action, including activities, timeline, resources, and evaluation checkpoints. Before you begin, collect baseline data to tell you where you are now. Then, collect follow-up data to see progress toward your goal after working your plan. It really is that simple. Charmaine had some preliminary data—her perception of the climate in her organization. She then used a reliable tool designed to afford confidentiality to collect further data. She knew that the success of these efforts required staff to be honest and trust that the process would not to cause them harm. From the mouth of leadership guru Peter Drucker, "What gets measured gets improved."

  There are other reasons to collect formal assessment data before you begin a program improvement plan:

  - Quick-fix solutions seldom work.
  - Data helps you distinguish the problem from the symptoms.
  - Data identifies and helps you build on what is going well.
  - Data promotes more objective decision making.
  - Formal data is needed to advocate for funding or other support.

- **Developing expertise in public relations and marketing:** The skill set for public relations and marketing is about effective external communications. A program leader must be able to communicate the program's philosophy and promote a positive public image not just to prospective families but also to business leaders, policy makers, and funders. Effective program leaders use social media, promotional literature, handbooks, newsletters, and press releases to communicate with a broad audience. Now that the scholarship program is underway, Charmaine is using social media to communicate about their Great Place to Work initiative. She has submitted a grant proposal to the local community foundation. She has reached out to several higher-education institutions to negotiate a discounted rate for tuition for her staff. Charmaine has communicated to enrolled families the efforts underway and has asked for their support.

- **Adopting an entrepreneurial focus:** An effective strategic leader has an entrepreneurial focus (Abel et al. 2017; Douglass 2017). This is true regardless of the legal or business structure of the early learning program. Being entrepreneurial is about starting or growing a business. This focus is important to increase your profit, if you operate under a taxpaying business model, or grow your program, if you operate under a nonprofit business model, to reach more children and families or improve the quality of your services. The following are the characteristics of entrepreneurship applicable to an early childhood program leader.
  - Passionate about early learning programs or services
  - Unafraid to take risks
  - Confident in self-efficacy skills
  - Disciplined to stay the course
  - Adaptable and flexible
  - Has marketing expertise in both business and strategic planning skills and in money-management skills

Charmaine demonstrates an entrepreneurial mindset. She is passionate about changing the organizational climate in her program and appears willing to work toward this goal for as long as it takes. She has strong marketing, planning, and money-management skills. Too often these tools are associated only with a business leader with a profit motivation. Early childhood program leaders of all stripes need these tools in their toolboxes.

Take-Away Strategies: Consensus Building with Your Staff

Consensus is a powerful method to use when you are making a decision that is strategic as opposed to operational in nature. Ask yourself whether the consequences of the decision will be long-lasting and/or expensive to implement (or reverse) or whether you need to be sure of the commitment of all stakeholders not to undermine the decision. Here are three simple ways to reach consensus:

- **Five-finger voting:** Stakeholders hold up their fingers depending on the degree to which they support the decision proposed.
  - Five fingers: indicates full agreement with the decision and enthusiastic support for its implementation
  - Four fingers: indicates agreement that it is a good decision and support for its implementation
  - Three fingers: indicates the decision is a good compromise and support for its implementation
  - Two fingers: indicates a lack of agreement but the voter will not sabotage the implementation
  - One finger: indicates no way—find another alternative
- **Rank order:** At times, a number of alternative choices are under consideration by a group. Stakeholders write each alternative on a piece of paper and then place them in order from most preferred to least preferred. Each placement has a numerical value. For example, if there are three alternatives, the one most preferred is given a value of three and the one least preferred is given a value of one. The points for each alternative are tallied to determine the best choice.
- **Dot voting:** Another way to reach consensus among group members who have generated multiple alternatives is to write the alternatives on flip-chart paper. Each stakeholder is given the same number of sticker dots (five to ten depending on the number of alternatives) with which to vote. Voters may put more than one sticker on any alternative, indicating the strength of their preference.

Boosting Advocacy Leadership

Charmaine is proud of what she has accomplished in her organization. The staff morale is on the rise; teachers are working to increase their qualifications and getting ready to apply for the state wage supplement. She is speaking at a city council meeting: "The low wages paid to staff are the result of a failed market-based approach to financing early care and education. We have learned so much about the developing brains of young children. We expect early educators to know how to support children's development and prepare them to thrive in school and throughout life. But the compensation of the early care and education workforce has not kept up with this new knowledge, increased responsibilities, and professional expectations. Parents can't afford to pay. Teachers can't afford to stay. There has to be a better way. We have to do something about compensation for the good of the children and families, as well as for the workforce."

Program leaders are in a unique position to practice advocacy as a basic responsibility of leadership. They can connect with other organizations and partners to strengthen their impact (Page et al. 2016). They need the tools—the knowledge and skills and dispositions—to advocate on behalf of linguistically, culturally, socioeconomically, and ability-diverse children and families. And they need these same tools to advocate on behalf of the profession.

Three approaches to advocacy leadership will get you started in using your influence effectively to strengthen the internal and external influence of your program. These include speaking out for children, families, staff, and programs; being aware of policies that affect children and families; and joining with others for greater impact.

- **Standing up and speaking out for children, families, staff, and programs:** Advocacy is about communication skills—verbal, nonverbal, and written. It is also about courage. As authors Susi Long, Mariana Souto-Manning, and Vivian Maria Vasquez (2016) note, "hopeful futures will not be realized without addressing injustices that prevail in schools and society . . . open hearts must be anchored in firm commitments to call out inequities and move deliberately to disrupt and dismantle them." Charmaine has carefully prepared her statement to the city council. She wrote her words carefully, getting her facts straight and the tone forceful but respectful. Then, she practiced in front of a mirror. No one present at the meeting would know how terrified Charmaine is of public speaking.

- **Being aware of public policies that affect children and families:** Compensation disparity among educators working in the different sectors of early childhood education—child care, Head Start, and public pre-K—is a systemic problem that requires a system-level solution. This disparity is the result of public policies. Charmaine is well-versed in how these public policies affect the well-being of young children and their families. Charmaine advocates for increased public investment in early care and education whenever there is an opportunity. At the city council meeting, Charmaine is advocating for support at the municipal level; she is making the case for the city to fund the infrastructure of a shared- services alliance.

> "One isn't necessarily born with courage, but one is born with potential. Without courage, we cannot practice any other virtue with consistency. We can't be kind, true, merciful, generous, or honest."
>
> —Maya Angelou

This innovative model would lower costs for early care and education organizations, and the savings would be directed to enhanced compensation for early educators.

- **Joining with others for greater impact:** The shared-services model is gaining momentum nationally. In a shared-services alliance there are cost savings for members based on economy of scale for business-related supplies and services. The early childhood directors' network has investigated what this model might look like in their city. Charmaine has joined with other program leaders who are enthusiastic about the potential of a shared-services alliance. They are eager to try a collective approach to increasing compensation for early childhood educators.

Developing Community Leadership

Charmaine reports back to the governing board of her organization: "I am thrilled that the city council has agreed to fund the start-up of a shared-services alliance. Now the work begins in earnest. Our goal is a model that can result in significant savings for the early childhood organizations that agree to direct these savings toward increases in staff compensation. Here is what has happened so far. The early childhood directors' network has engaged a consultant and invited other community organizations, city agencies, and the chamber of commerce to a forum to learn about the shared-services alliance model. We are hoping to have a big turnout and get the support of the business community as well."

Charmaine has put into place the two pillars of community leadership: identifying strengths and assets and collaborating with partners across systems. She understands her role in making connections to others and aligning goals that can affect all aspects of systems to improve outcomes for children and their families. The following are the skills you can use to increase your influence in community leadership.

- **Knowing the strengths and assets within your community:** Charmaine is connected to her community. She attends events sponsored by local community organizations such as the library, park district, and chamber of commerce. She is an early childhood ambassador for the United Way campaign each year. In this capacity, she goes out to speak to businesses about how their contributions to United Way help early childhood organizations in the community serve disadvantaged children and families. Charmaine is a leader in the local early childhood professional community. She serves as the advocate for the early childhood directors' network.

- **Collaborating with community partners across systems of education, health, and family support:** Charmaine connects with the health department, the public elementary-school district, and social-service agencies on a regular basis. She knows who to go to when she needs support or resources to meet the needs of the children and families in her program. Charmaine tells families during the new-family orientation meeting, "It takes a village to raise a child, especially when you live in a city." The invitation to the forum on shared services was sent to each of the principals of the elementary schools in the district, district-level administrators of support services, as well as to key staff in city agencies. Charmaine is convinced it will take collaboration across systems for the shared-services alliance to be most successful.

⛏ Digging Deeper: Using Standards and Tools to Improve Administrative Leadership

Ensuring that your organization is a great place to learn for children and a great place to work for staff will include a systematic and comprehensive review of the leadership and management practices in your program. This task can be made easier by using guidance provided in the following research-based resources.

- NAEYC Accreditation Standard 10—Leadership and Management

  Whether you are embarking on a comprehensive plan to improve organizational climate or just want to update or your family handbook, a good place to start is the *NAEYC Early Learning Program Accreditation Standards and Assessment Items*. Each topic area provides a description and recommended best practices. This resource will provide valuable insights to improve the leadership and management of your program. This authoritative reference includes six topic areas. You and your staff should explore these items in detail.

  - Leadership
  - Management Policies and Procedures
  - Fiscal Accountability Policies and Procedures
  - Health, Nutrition, and Safety Policies and Procedures
  - Personnel Policies
  - Program Evaluation, Accountability, and Continuous Improvement

- *Program Administration Scale (PAS): Measuring Early Childhood Leadership and Management*, 2nd edition

  The PAS is premised on the belief that early childhood program quality should be viewed through a broader lens than only the classroom learning environment. High-quality interactions and learning environments at the classroom level cannot be sustained unless there are high-quality practices at the organizational level (Talan and Bloom 2011). The PAS, which is designed to reliably assess and improve leadership and management practices at the center level, has twenty-five items comprised of 316 indicators of quality. You and your staff can use the indicators to incrementally improve your leadership and management practices and benchmark your progress over time.

⚙ What Works Best: Knowing Why Administrative Leadership Matters

There is a growing body of research on the relationship of administrative leadership to the quality of early childhood programs and the quality of the work environment.

- Research has established a positive relationship between the quality of administrative practices and the quality of the children's learning environment in center-based programs (Dennis and O'Connor 2013; Ackerman and Sansanelli 2010; Lower and Cassidy 2007).

- A study from the Urban Institute in Washington, DC, suggests that when programs are more secure financially, they are more likely to have higher expectations for teachers and are better able to support staff (Rohacek et al. 2010). In addition, this study shows that when site leaders have hands-on involvement with creating the budget, as opposed to just receiving it, they experience lower financial stress. This factor is associated with higher observed classroom quality.

- Research also suggests that directors with higher levels of education and specialized training in program administration are more likely to support the professional development of their teaching staff, secure and maintain program funding, and achieve center accreditation (Ackerman 2008; Mims et al. 2008).

- An important body of research shows the relationship between teacher retention and the quality of the work environment (Totenhagen et al. 2016). In a study of Head Start and Early Head Start teaching staff, workplace satisfaction, which includes the perceived relationship between teaching staff and the director, predict actual turnover (Wells 2015).

Chapter 8 Study Guide: Putting Administrative Leadership into Practice

Operational Leadership

One of the cores of administrative leadership is operational leadership. Developing staff and overseeing operations are critical aspects of administrative practice. As you read the following scenario, consider how leadership essentials, administrative leadership, and pedagogical practices support these practices. Label each example according to its leadership component: **LE** for leadership essentials, **AL** for administrative leadership, and **PL** for pedagogical leadership. Note: some examples may demonstrate more than one component.

When Tessa, the director of Creative Learning for Little Ones, is promoted from teacher to director, she decides to make some changes. After facilitating her first staff meeting, she quickly learns that this is more difficult than it seemed when she was a participant. She decides to include information about staff meetings in the orientation for the next new person she hires.

Tessa adds a section titled "Participation in Meetings" to the employee handbook. It describes the importance of participating fully in meetings. She includes expectations such coming prepared, being invested in content, voicing thoughts, and contributing to discussions. She adds reflecting, sharing opinions, questioning, staying on task, and appreciating the perspectives of others. Finally, she adds taking responsibility to contribute in different roles during meetings. Tessa outlines the importance of the active-participant role in making decisions, ensuring the mission of the center is considered, ensuring various viewpoints are represented, and encouraging innovative thought. She feels these additions reflect the core beliefs and values of the program.

As a result of the mediocre participation during her first staff meeting, Tessa decides to intentionally involve staff in different ways. She recognizes that Barbara is very creative, so she asks her to create a warm-up activity that will encourage conversation among the group. She knows that Robyn is doing a college project on transitions in classrooms, so she invites her to share some strategies with staff.

When Tessa facilitates the next staff meeting, she is clear about norms and expectations. One week before the meeting, she creates a draft agenda and emails it to staff asking them to review the agenda items and send other topics to be discussed. Two staff members make suggestions. She responds and asks them to facilitate the discussion on the topics they submitted. She meets with them to offer support as they design their sections of the meeting. She encourages them to read about meeting facilitation and follows up by giving them an article on the topic. Additional staff ask to participate more in meetings and desire coaching on meeting facilitation. Tessa incorporates this into their professional development plan and addresses it during reflective-supervision meetings. As a result, staff create a peer-learning group to support one another in this role. Tessa provides self-assessments on leadership style and communication skills. She asks staff to complete a survey about meeting purpose, structure, and follow-up. After staff complete the survey, they discuss ideas for improving meetings. One staff member attends a conference session to learn more about how to facilitate with finesse. Eventually, facilitating at staff meetings becomes a criterion for the lead teacher position and is added to the job description.

At the end of the year Catie, one of the teachers, meets with Tessa to reflect on the year. She shares how much she has grown through this process and how Tessa's support, encouragement, and willingness to share personal examples of success and opportunities for improvement have been instrumental in her ability to take risks and grow.

Review the labels you added in the scenario. If you were to remove the sections you labeled with **AL**, how would that affect the likelihood that meetings would be successful?

_____

_____

_____

_____

_____

_____

_____

_____

_____

What will happen if you remove the **PL** or **LE** labels?

_____

_____

_____

_____

_____

_____

_____

_____

_____

_____

_____

When leadership essentials, administrative leadership, and pedagogical leadership are integrated, organizations are more likely to be successful as the practices support the functions of the other areas. The connections among each component create an environment where what is preached is not only practiced but is substantiated with structures and policies that help ensure effective and efficient work takes place.

Leveraging Your Leadership Qualities

Cultivating a Clear Vision

> Parents Teresa and Bob laugh sympathetically as they exit the building toward the parking lot. "It's hard getting up early, but it jump-starts my day to see my children so happy." Teresa adds, "Becca and Ellie love to come and hate to leave. At the end of the day, they ask to stay and play."
>
> Bob agrees. "We're lucky to have such a strong program. The teachers are great role models for our children."

In this thriving program, staff greet each other with genuine enthusiasm. The buzz of warm conversation and peaceful but lively activities in classrooms are evident to all who enter. Children hug their friends on arrival. Parents know each other by name and enjoy informal conversations. In the afternoon, they linger to talk about their day and about upcoming program activities. Throughout the organization, staff, families, and children experience a sense of familiarity and belonging.

This was Joanna's dream—to lead a program in which families feel at home and children can thrive. In ten years of leadership, she has seen children grow up, new siblings enter, and families recommend the program to friends. Joanna wants her workplace to exemplify quality early care and education. She wants people to make and remember positive experiences and to leave each day with a sense of confidence that children are receiving all they need to reach their full potential.

This program has embraced the Whole Leadership Framework. Joanna has included the framework in the staff handbook and displays it on the wall in her office. Joanna wants staff and families to know how early childhood program leadership is understood and shared within the program. The framework helps her bring people together around a common vision and inspires commitment and active engagement in the program.

With the Whole Leadership Framework as a guide, you will be prepared to talk about the unique strengths and needs of your particular families and community. You can share your values and mission with new families and with external stakeholders and collaborators in the community. While your approach will be unique to your neighborhood, culture, and philosophical goals, the framework will help you adapt your leadership priorities to best serve your program. You will be able to communicate your ongoing commitment to professionalism and be effective as you create a high-impact program.

The framework provides a guide to visualize the way various parts of the organization affect other areas of work. For example, when you change approaches to teaching, how will you involve families in decision making and update them on progress? When you revise the program handbook, how will you communicate these differences to staff and to families? When you embrace a positive-guidance approach, how can you be sure that all in the program have the needed skills to be successful? When you make changes to food purchases or supplies, how will staff manage these changes? From a practical perspective, the framework will help you connect and integrate daily decisions into the larger effects they will have on the whole organization.

Above all, the Whole Leadership Framework will help you highlight the elements of your program that positively influence the growth and development of children. It presents the integrated aspects of leadership that, together, can maximize your investment and strengthen needed resources to achieve your goals. The more you understand the functional aspects of your work and how they fit together, the more you will make informed and effective decisions.

Fueling Continuous Quality Improvement

Annette invites Barrett's parents, Josh and Shana, into her preschool classroom. "We're excited about science play. Look how Barrett used the materials to construct a windmill. He used the pictures in this book to guide his ideas. Our program focuses on science, technology, engineering, and math, and our director has provided a STEM coach to support innovative teaching in these areas. We are delighted to see the way children respond."

Josh replies, "Barrett has been talking nonstop about his building project. It's exciting to see what he is learning."

Annette has planned conferences for several weeks and is delighted to share the science unit with families. This unit focuses on wind. Children have experimented with blowing materials and have explored books about windmills.

For the past year, Sasha, the director of the program, has invested program resources to bring developmentally appropriate science investigations into the toddler and preschool classrooms. She applied for a small grant to fund a STEM coach, who has helped teachers evaluate materials and plan age-appropriate activities and events. While the visible goal was to intensify learning opportunities for children, Sasha had another motive in jump-starting this project. She had noticed that teachers just weren't as engaged in their professional growth as she had hoped. By identifying a project that all staff could work on together across age levels, the spirit of engagement in teaching was reenergized.

In addition to encouraging teaching staff to share ideas with families, Sasha has highlighted the science, technology, engineering, and math focus in the program newsletter. When teaching staff attend conferences or the coach works with the program staff, she highlights the professional learning experiences on the social-media page. As staff complete courses or earn certificates, she gives generous kudos and announces the achievement on the program website. These efforts communicate a vital sense of growth and excellence that are embodied in program commitments and actions.

Ongoing growth is necessary for professional excellence, and the Whole Leadership Framework will serve as a guide to program improvement. You can use the framework for reflection and insight about administration and management and can explore priorities for pedagogical growth. Leadership essentials can draw your attention to the personal, interpersonal, and professional growth that will support a positive organizational climate and program success. The three areas of whole leadership will help you review immediate needs and set action steps for yourself, with coaches, and with staff. Over time, you will be able to use this information to set long-term goals and implement positive action steps that lead to noticeable positive change.

As you participate in quality-improvement efforts, you may invite a coach or subject-matter expert who can talk with you about areas of your program that can be strengthened. Like Sasha's, your effort may involve teachers, or it may be part of your own investment in leadership learning. Quality-improvement efforts may also involve greater collaboration and involvement with community leaders and organizations. Perhaps you will want to partner with other directors to focus on learning about a particular area or priority.

⚙ What Works Best: Why Leadership Is Essential for Quality Improvement

Guiding professional growth and program improvement is a key leadership responsibility. Quality in the classroom begins with a safe and stimulating setting; however, positive outcomes for children are dependent on high-quality interactions among teachers and children. The capability of teachers to deliver these high-quality practices consistently depends on their education, professional development, and ongoing support. Equally important are the organizational supports—paid curriculum planning time, reflective supervision, and a community of practice with peers—that undergird effective teaching and that depend on the program leader's commitment to quality.

Teachers' ability to engage in high-quality interactions depends a great deal on organizational features such as leadership (Pianta et al. 2016). Workplace climate and teachers' sense of positive community contribute to instructional quality and to children's language and learning (Guo et al. 2011). A sense of community is a positive predicator of quality when teachers feel empowered and involved in organizational decisions (McGinty et al. 2008). For these reasons, fostering a climate of active participation and growth is essential.

Program leaders must "take initiative to actively and intentionally create site-specific environments that support and nurture meaningful, satisfying, and intellectually challenging professional growth" (Jaruszewicz and White 2009). Program directors can intentionally establish positive growing conditions through commitment to professional development, ensuring intellectual safety and challenge, creative use of resources, respect for all stakeholders, and intentional modeling. Understanding the connection between leadership and the experiences of teachers and children is essential. Directors' leadership skills and administrative practices have a significant effect on classroom quality and a long-term influence on the health and effectiveness of a program (Doherty et al. 2015).

Responsive teachers support children's individual needs, use proactive behavior guidance, and are intentional about fostering language and cognitive development (Hamre et al. 2014; Masterson and Kersey 2013). They display emotional warmth and ongoing support for skill development during teaching and behavior guidance. These interactions are highly dependent on teachers' background knowledge, training and skills but also involve their mood and stress level (Jeon et al. 2018). They need support for stress management along with accurate feedback and accountability for classroom interaction quality.

Program leaders must facilitate professional well-being and learning for staff by providing curriculum resources and materials, encouraging teachers to engage in systematic growth, and facilitating participation in quality rating and improvement initiatives. All of these leadership ingredients contribute to ongoing quality improvement.

⊠ Take-Away Strategies: Fostering Effective Learning

Whether you are preparing for staff meetings or job-embedded learning experiences, making the most of the resources you have is a critical skill. Use the following questions to reflect on past activities and plan for those ahead:

- Was the event, meeting, or activity productive, meaningful, and effective for all present?
- What could I have done ahead of time to make this interaction more productive, meaningful, and/or effective?
- What could others have done to prepare for, contribute to, or respond to this interaction to make it more productive, meaningful, and effective?
- Were there sufficient technology resources, information handouts, time for discussion, and/or materials to support desired results?
- What follow-up is useful or necessary? For example, could you make a phone call or send a summary email? Would additional information or training be helpful? Would it help to explore a related topic? What are the next action steps?
- What could I have done and what will I plan to do in the future to communicate more effectively?
- Are there resources, such as books, videos, handouts, and articles, which will provide additional information?
- Do the questions or concerns raised point to follow-up topics that need to be addressed?
- Was there sufficient interest or need to suggest creating an ongoing learning community or applied classroom strategies related to this topic?

Building on Community Partnerships and Resources

> Shanice and Maynard arrive early to set up tables. Members of the parent board, along with organization leaders from the community, set out materials for the family night. "I am so proud of the work we have done to make this possible," says Lauren, the executive director.
>
> "Yes, our second annual community celebration has made a difference," responds Maynard. "I love our racing theme and the motto, 'A better start in life.'"
>
> Shanice adds, "This is a wonderful time for the teachers to get to know families and to explore community resources."

This event is the result of months of planning. A group of families began meeting regularly with the parent board to talk about ways to connect with the community. They decided to host a fall kick-off event and invite nonprofit organizations, the park district, local elementary schools, and community health professionals. Those who contribute to this evening's event set up tables with materials that feature educational and health services. They answer questions and stay to talk with families. Families come to hear a presentation about school readiness by a local child-development specialist.

Planning this event didn't require superhero skills. Lauren had a sincere desire to do something innovative, something that would make a difference to enrolled families and connect them to the larger community. It took some time to consider the possibilities and to bring this vision to life.

Lauren and the program board wanted to move from being a provider of early care and education to an organization with a new level of impact. They wanted to become a lively and thriving learning organization that could connect families to the community and better prepare children for school and a successful life.

Leading an early childhood program is not a solo sport. You need and depend on the insights, wisdom, and contributions of all who work for and participate in your organization. The relationships you have with others provide perspective and balance to your daily work. Are there other ways for you to use your resources and time? Is the program making progress toward its goals? Have you missed a critical need that should be addressed? Others who know you and your organization well can provide critical feedback to help you accurately appraise the needs of your program, its current impact, and its potential.

Take-Away Strategies: Inviting Communication

Open communication within your organization is critical to your knowledge of the needs and perspectives of stakeholders. Parent boards, family support groups, and regular staff meetings are a good place to start. A mindset of active engagement can energize your program.

- Hold weekly touch-base meetings with members of your staff to ask for honest feedback.
- Let families and staff know when and how you can be contacted and when you are available to talk. Invite their ideas for the program.
- Hold focus groups with teachers or families, and present specific questions for feedback.
- Offer monthly coffee groups for families, with specific topics for discussion.
- Hold jump-start meetings with teachers to set specific goals and track progress.
- Invite staff to add items to your staff-meeting agenda, and provide adequate time for discussion.
- With board members and other stakeholders, brainstorm new ways to develop and improve your program.
- When challenges occur, ask for input from all involved: "What is a good way to solve this problem?" "What resources or information do we need?" "What else can we be doing to address this need?"
- Ask families, staff, and board members to contribute to blogs or newsletter columns that highlight their work or innovative ideas and practices.

In addition to building internal connections, set aside at least one morning a month to meet with community leaders who can provide an outside perspective. What issues are affecting children in your community? Who can be a support to your organization? Who will be a good thought partner? Who can contribute innovative ideas and solutions to the challenges you face? Get to know your mayor, chief of police, local pediatricians, park district supervisor, librarian, early intervention specialists, quality-improvement coaches, other program directors, school principals, human-service organization leaders, and others invested in early childhood development and education. External perspectives are richly informative and can provide you with the spark for your next great idea.

Focusing only on the day-to-day work within your program can narrow your circle of focus and diminish your sphere of influence. By building relationships, you gain a strong and balanced perspective about the importance of your work and its integration with other community services for children. The more you are involved, the more you will see opportunities for partnerships, collaboration, shared events, and the potential for funding opportunities. You will discover opportunities to promote your program and to learn about services and events that can benefit your children and families. Importantly, you will discover your dependence on others for professional interaction, meaningful connections, and information.

Sharing the Whole Leadership Framework with others will help you illustrate and communicate about the work of your program and its priorities. Without this framework as an anchor, others may hold various notions about what you do. They may see you solely as a small-business owner, a child-care provider, a supervisor of teachers, or as a principal of a school. The Whole Leadership Framework will help you communicate the way all functions of your work are necessary to effective leadership. The visual picture will align and integrate the many views of early care and education and will ground your conversations in professionalism. It will help other people understand your goals and better see the complex ways that your work is integrated.

Active engagement with the community not only strengthens external resources and partnerships but also gives you professional credibility with your staff. They will see you as a role model and leader, actively representing the work of your program with others. They will hear about your advocacy for children in your community and see you advancing the professionalism of the field. They will take greater pride and ownership in their work, knowing they are part of a purpose larger than their program. They will be able to embrace their work as part of larger community-wide effort to meet the needs of children and families.

As an active participant with community health and service agencies, you will gain the latest knowledge about prenatal care physical and mental health and wellness. You will learn from literacy and library specialists about the critical need to support children's developing language and cognitive growth both at home and in early childhood programs. Importantly, you will be able to better highlight children's need for consistent security with their caregivers in the context of safe neighborhoods and high-quality programs and schools. These circles of support work prepare children for a strong start in life.

You must bring your greater purpose and mission into focus on a daily basis, highlighting the reasons for the work you do, emphasizing the developmental needs of the whole child in the context of family and community. Staff are more likely to invest in continuous growth and get involved in community efforts when they recognize the impact of their work on children's future school and life success.

Maximizing Human Capacity and Shared Positive Culture

Zinnia reflects with Jason about his work in the classroom. She asks, "How did things go yesterday? Did you get the materials organized?"

Jason responds, "It meant a lot that you took time to look at my room with me. Your suggestions were helpful. I asked Paula to help me move shelves, and we added bins to sort materials."

"That's terrific," Zinnia says. "If you decide you want to order the cart or need additional containers, just let me know."

As a program leader you have a daily influence on the lives of your staff and families. The comments you make when teachers meet with you affect their sense of competence. The support you give (or withhold) to their plans can either motivate or discourage them. Zinnia is meeting with each staff member to make a room-improvement plan, and the results so far have been terrific. Each teacher has planned small steps that have positively affected their teaching. The changes have made a difference in the way they experience their director's support, as well.

No influence is more important than the one you have on staff. They look for you to mentor and support their growth. They want to be part of a meaningful profession and participate in a program that values their contributions and effort. They need positive relationships and want to experience a sense of connection and belonging. They want to feel respected and know that their work makes a difference.

Families also are influenced by your leadership. Their confidence in the program and sense of belonging are affected by their interactions with you. Their children are their greatest investment. Early education experiences can influence the way families feel for years to come about relating to schools and their perceptions about the kind of support they will receive. Parents' views of their children as capable, thriving, and happy provide reassurance. Confidence in your program contributes to the stability of the family system.

Leaders often spend a great deal of time focusing on managing budgets, schedules, physical structures, and events. These pressing tasks can, at times, feel overwhelming. Taking time to focus on the interpersonal dynamics of an organization, however, is essential to its effectiveness and impact.

What Works Best: Understanding the Impact of Leadership

Leadership involves understanding the ways people make meaning through relationships at work. It requires insight about the ways complex personal dynamics affect all other aspects of work effectiveness (Toytok and Kapusuzoglu 2015). Positive climate can be seen in the collegiality and physical setting of a work environment; in the way supervisors relate to staff; in role clarity and goal consensus; and in staff perceptions of shared decision making, program innovativeness, and a fair reward system (Bloom 2016). Creativity, innovation, and the ability of staff to embrace change are influenced by the way staff observe and perceive a leader's behavior (Isaksen and Akkermans 2011). The quality and nature of your relationships have a significant impact.

Organizational culture includes the values, assumptions, and beliefs of a program and results in a workplace that "recognizes, addresses, and celebrates the good work of staff—a work environment that welcomes laughter, collegiality, and freedom to innovate" (Bloom and Abel 2015). It is represented in the traditions and symbols that reflect a shared history. The climate is what staff experience as members of the organization (Dennis and O'Connor 2013). When program culture nurtures development and provides psychological safety and support, staff more readily embrace change and positive growth (Wanless 2016; Wanless and Winters 2018).

Some aspects of your work are nonnegotiable. Culturally and linguistically responsive practice is essential, no matter where your program is located. Organizational cultures may differ, so it is up to you to make visible expectations or barriers that might distance or exclude some members of your program. When families with differing linguistic needs participate in your program, connect them with community resources and, when needed, provide a cultural broker—someone who can act as a liaison and help them communicate their needs and questions and who can convey responsibilities involved in program participation. Involving families in open communication about caregiving is foundational and promotes child development. These aspects of ethical practice are mandatory and require purposeful attention, evaluation, and review.

Other aspects of leadership are negotiable. For example, you may have read about leadership styles or different approaches or theories of leadership. You may recognize there are multiple ways to support others and ensure responsibilities are completed. You must assess your own strengths and abilities and at the same time evaluate the needs of your staff. You must consider the history and resources of your program and community to make the most of their strengths. Just as a teacher connects to children's background knowledge, provides support for substantial growth, and addresses all areas of development, your responsibility is to adapt your ways of being to strengthen and build up the skills of your staff and families (Campion 2018).

The Whole Leadership Framework's leadership essentials empower your effectiveness. These are the qualities that make you effective as a leader. These traits first must be modeled and embraced fully in your own professional life, so that others see and understand your values. Your strong self-efficacy, active reflection of empathy, creativity, authenticity, humility, transparency, and adaptability will be evident to others as organizational norms. Your goal as a leader is to identify and build the strengths of your staff and to unify their work around the program mission and goals. As you embrace vital growth, others will see that continuous learning is needed for all who work with children. Leadership essentials help you identify and make the most of your own strengths and maximize the strengths, capabilities, and resources of your organization.

0⚷ Legacy of Leadership: Words and Actions Tell a Story

"What you bring to a situation, you also bring out in others. When you approach conversations with positivity and trust, you are more likely to receive the same in return. When you convey stable emotions and a sense of secure calm, others feel reassured. When you communicate words of sincere greeting, you put others at ease. Your words and actions tell a story about you."

Connecting Children and Families with Needed Resources

Celina Marie is the director of an early learning program located in a high school. She points to the page in a community resource guide that has a list of pediatric and adult health services. She says, "I know this practice is close to your home. Rowen will love the setting and kindness of the staff. They have a wall of books he will enjoy. They offer a family support group that other parents here have recommended."

Dionne replies, "Thank you. It has been hard since Rowen's father died. I really appreciate the support. Mrs. Lozano and the children in Rowen's class have been so loving and kind. The picnic was really special."

This director encourages staff to foster a sense of belonging among families. The resource manual conveys much more than factual information about the local community and opportunities for children. The smiling families depicted in the photographs reflect the special places and experiences of former families. The care and time Celina Marie has taken to compile and summarize the services shows her investment in and commitment to families. She feels strongly about connecting families with opportunities and resources.

Advocating for the needs of families means working toward a goal that can make a difference (Page et al. 2016). This work begins in your program by ensuring that teachers and other staff know the children well. Staff must have the vision to create the highest quality setting for children and must communicate to others the importance of issues that affect children directly: prenatal care, secure attachments, consistency of caregiving, and continued access to nutrition and healthcare for young children and families. This work means hiring and supporting program staff who are committed to practices that nurture and empower children's development and learning to the fullest.

Advocacy at the program level means honoring and valuing the strengths and contributions of family members and collaborating with them to coordinate responsive nurture and care. Advocacy also includes promoting universal early developmental screenings that can ensure children get off to a strong start. It means you and your staff make connections to secure needed supports and services for young children. You make sure staff learn about, participate in, and support home-visiting programs for infants and toddlers. As part of your program mission, you seek to offer strong networking and educational opportunities for families.

Outside your center, you can invest time and resources in the areas of child development that are important to you. Perhaps you want to support an early literacy effort, participate in infant and toddler mental-health organizations, or contribute your time and skills to special-needs initiatives in your local community. You may have a background in the visual or performing arts or music or have cultural and language interests that will draw you to local service.

Find local government, educational organizations, and civic groups that sponsor fundraisers, educational events, and town-hall meetings to bring together stakeholders. You can explore opportunities by finding out all you can about nonprofit organizations that are serving children in your community. Once you are involved, you will add to your understanding about the ways your state systems and policies impact the needs of local children and families.

At the state level, contact your legislator to share your personal story of investment in early education. Advocate for programs and strategies that secure funding and educational opportunities for children and families, especially in high-need areas. Make yourself aware of legislation and funding that affect children and families both where you live as well as nationally.

As much as advocacy requires speaking out whenever possible for children and families, advocacy also requires staying informed about issues that affect the profession. Learn all you can about your state quality improvement system and state affiliate for NAEYC or the National Association for Family Child Care. Attend conferences where you can connect with others to strengthen your advocacy knowledge and voice.

The McCormick Center for Early Childhood Leadership offers a national conference for early childhood leaders that can connect you with a network of highly committed professionals already active in speaking on behalf of young children and their families, the early childhood workforce, and the need for greater investment in the quality of early childhood programs. They prioritize issues of equity and access to high-quality care and promote professional competencies and learning opportunities for the field of early childhood leadership. They can support your efforts to become a powerful change agent in the lives of children and families.

🪏 Digging Deeper: Embracing Advocacy

The contribution you can make to child advocacy is a strong and vibrant program. Roger Neugebauer (2016) suggests that advocacy includes building your program's reputation, maintaining high enrollment, securing outside resources, uniting the early childhood profession, educating the public about the importance of the early years, and advocating for sound public policies. It is important to consider that advocacy includes all aspects of your work and profession. Start by inviting your staff to envision an advocacy project in your program, community, or state. Together, you can explore organizations, initiatives, and policies that impact the profession.

- Sign up for McCormick Center for Early Childhood Leadership emails and social media, to stay informed on policy happenings and needs in early childhood leadership. See https://mccormickcenter.nl.edu

- Subscribe to NAEYC Power to the Profession communications, to stay current about workforce policies, initiatives, and data that relate to professional compensation and training. See www.naeyc.org/profession

- Explore the BUILD Initiative and learn about state-systems work and quality-improvement initiatives that can inform your work. See: www.buildinitiative.org

- Find resources and information at Zero to Three to strengthen your work with infant and toddler development. See: www.zerotothree.org

Putting It All Together to Increase Your Impact

> "These are beautiful," Kristie comments as she smells the flowers.
>
> "And the chocolate is a nice touch," adds Rossella. "It's nice to have everything ready. It's a good morning when I can smell the coffee."
>
> "I agree," says Bill. He pours himself a second cup. "My brain works better when it is caffeinated."

Jill works well with the assistant director, Hannah, to plan staff-development experiences. She knows the needs of her teaching staff and has put together an interactive activity on language development and literacy. Jill depends on Hannah to edit and copy materials and to set up the room for training. Hannah likes preparing the setting and feels rewarded when others enjoy the event. She knows the physical setting can be as important in a learning experience as the activities.

Some people see themselves as "big picture" visionaries and others prefer to be "in the weeds" as they manage and attend to daily responsibilities. Your effectiveness depends on your ability to take on multiple perspectives and to do so well. To make informed decisions, you need to see and understand what is really happening and consider the effects on all stakeholders. This requires your focus on the organization as a whole as well as your detailed attention to the minor details. The Whole Leadership Framework can help you move from the macro (big picture) to the micro (intricate details) perspective and envision the parts of the whole as an integrated system.

A daily scan of the framework can bring to your attention to areas that are neglected or that need some serious revision, as well as point out areas of strength. As a leader, you need to communicate your priorities to staff so there is transparency about your work and time. Otherwise, they may see you as being behind a black curtain and not understand your priorities, projects, and challenges. Using the visual framework at staff meetings can help you explain the importance of the individual pieces of your work, as well as how those pieces fit together.

As you set goals, you can use the Whole Leadership Framework to make shared or distributed leadership visible. You ask, "How does what we do today affect children now and later? Are our program goals clearly stated? Have staff participated in forming these goals and given feedback about these goals? Have we used each area of the Whole Leadership Framework to be sure our work is thriving and vital? Are we using all of our resources most effectively?" The resulting conversations will provide fruitful feedback to guide future discussions and planning.

In the same way, staff who understand their own work context will be more informed to ask questions, offer support, and recognize the importance of their contributions to a particular area of whole leadership. The whole leadership conceptual framework can help staff see how individuals within the program contribute competencies, skills, and dispositions. They contribute needed insights about the program and its impact on children and families. This inside-outside approach is critical to the health of a complex organization that serves people with multiple perspectives and changing needs. Without a scaffolding structure for thinking, planning, and communication, your success and effectiveness as an interconnected group of individuals will be, at best, hit or miss.

Most importantly, the framework can help you identify areas for your own growth and development. The competencies of your state's administrator credential can be aligned with the framework. Administrative leadership, pedagogical leadership, and leadership essentials can provide an overarching framework for your professional-development planning to help you stay on track.

The framework can guide your participation in national organizations, as you add new information to your toolbox and increase your competence as a program leader. Finally, as you advocate on behalf of the early childhood education system, the framework can guide conversations with funders and policy makers about the need for comprehensive leadership development.

Take-Away Strategies: Using the Whole Leadership Framework for Meaningful Reflection

As you view the tools for pedagogical and administrative leadership and leadership essentials, the following questions can guide your reflection and planning.

Identifying needs

- In what aspects of work do you spend the most time daily? weekly?
- What activities require the most psychological and physical energy?
- What aspects of your work do you find most stressful or draining?
- In which aspects of work do you find you are missing skills or knowledge?
- Which areas of work do you feel need more attention?
- What areas of work require major reinforcement or support?
- In what area would you like to improve or invest additional learning and effort?

Identifying strengths

- Which areas of work do you look forward to daily? weekly?
- Which parts of work focus and activity energize and excite you?
- What aspects of work are going smoothly or need only minor tweaking?
- In what areas of work do you want to invest additional time, because you find them rewarding?
- In what areas do you function well as a role model to staff and families?
- What human and physical resources are present that can be used more effectively?

Evaluating interactions

- What are you doing well for and with families?
- What feedback have you received from families about program policies and events?
- How have you responded and what action steps have you taken as a result of family feedback?
- What would you like to see happen in your interactions with others outside of the organization in your community and state?
- What would you like to see happen in your interactions with others through professional involvement?
- In what area can you create a training or share your knowledge with others?

To foster a mindset of creativity and innovation, the Whole Leadership Framework provides a picture of the ways internal and external resources strengthen your program. Rather than being impermeable or rigid, the framework represents a living organization of the many aspects of leadership work. It presents the full scope of leadership influences that can have multidirectional effects. At the same time, it illustrates the way leadership is informed by and makes use of internal and external resources —both physical and human—to strengthen its effectiveness.

The Whole Leadership Framework connects the leadership of your organization with its contribution to the community, support systems for children, the economic viability of your state, and the strength and vitality of the country. As you prepare children with skills for learning and foster their development within the context of their families and communities, you make a lasting impact on their future. All of this is possible because of the stability and ongoing growth of your program.

To ensure the continuity and effectiveness of your program over time, the Whole Leadership Framework will help you maximize your leadership and influence within and outside of your organization. With the support and collaboration of others, you will make a lasting contribution to the lives of children and families and add to the impressive history and legacy of early childhood education.

Chapter 9 Study Guide: Adopting the Whole Leadership Framework

Whole Leadership: A Framework to Guide Your Vision

This book provides you with strategies to develop a program anchored in the foundation of the Whole Leadership Framework. By creating a program that values the three components of whole leadership, you are more likely to sustain quality in the present and move your program forward to a healthy and thriving future. You have seen the integrated and reciprocal relationships among leadership essentials, administrative leadership, and pedagogical leadership, which can be used to reframe and revitalize your vision.

A *vision* is defined in the *Program Administration Scale* as "a statement of an ideal that can be used to motive, inspire, and guide [a leader] toward a future state" (Talan and Bloom 2011). Write a vision statement that reflects your commitment to embedding the Whole Leadership Framework in your program.

_____

_____

_____

_____

_____

By adopting the Whole Leadership Framework, you recognize that continuous improvements are vital to the growth and sustainability of your program. In your leadership role, what actions will you take to create a norm of continuous quality improvement among the staff?

_____

_____

_____

_____

_____

Building Whole Leadership by Building on Community Partnerships

Review the Whole Leadership Framework on page 3. What local organizations and external community resources are available to help you grow in each domain? Generate a list in the spaces provided.

Leadership Essentials	Administrative Leadership	Pedagogical Leadership

Every Interaction Counts

Reflect on your interactions with staff and families in the past week. Provide three examples of positive interactions.

_____

_____

_____

_____

Was it easy or difficult to think of examples? How you interact with others is a determining factor for how people feel about your organization. What three actions will you take this week to foster a positive organizational climate?

_____

_____

_____

_____

Interdependence: The Critical Element

Complete the following schedule with your typical tasks for the week.

Time	Monday	Tuesday	Wednesday	Thursday	Friday
7:00 a.m.–7:30 a.m.					
7:30 a.m.–8:00 a.m.					
8:00 a.m.–8:30 a.m.					
8:30 a.m.–9:00 a.m.					
9:00 a.m.–9:30 a.m.					
9:30 a.m.–10:00 a.m.					
10:00 a.m.–10:30 a.m.					
10:30 a.m.–11:00 a.m.					
11:00 a.m.–11:30 a.m.					
11:30 a.m.–12:00 p.m.					
12:00 p.m.–12:30 p.m.					
12:30 p.m.–1:00 p.m.					
1:00 p.m.–1:30 p.m.					
1:30 p.m.–2:00 p.m.					
2:00 p.m.–2:30 p.m.					
2:30 p.m.–3:00 p.m.					
3:00 p.m.–3:30 p.m.					
3:30 p.m.–4:00 p.m.					
4:00 p.m.–4:30 p.m.					
4:30 p.m.–5:00 p.m.					
5:00 p.m.–5:30 p.m.					
5:30 p.m.–6:00 p.m.					
6:00 p.m.–6:30 p.m.					

Next, review your schedule through the whole leadership lens. Note how frequently you spend time participating in and completing tasks related to each domain: leadership essentials, administrative leadership, and pedagogical leadership. As you scan your schedule, answer the following questions.

- How you spend your time reflects what you value. If your schedule does not seem to fit that notion, how can you restructure your days to allow time in your week to reflect your values?
- Organizations are more successful when there is a balance among the three domains of whole leadership. Keep in mind that leadership tasks can be shared, even as you exercise program leadership in each of the domains. As you evaluate your schedule and those of other leaders in your organization, do you feel there is a balance among domains? If not, what steps can you take to create an integrated balance?

Unintended Consequences

What are the consequences of having a program with a strong emphasis in administrative leadership, but not pedagogical leadership, or vice versa?

- Consequences of a **strong** emphasis in administrative leadership but a **weak** emphasis on pedagogical leadership

---

- Consequences of a **weak** emphasis in both administrative leadership and pedagogical leadership

---

- Consequences of a **strong** emphasis in pedagogical leadership but a **weak** emphasis on administrative leadership

---

- Consequences of a **strong** emphasis in both pedagogical leadership and administrative leadership

---

How do leadership essentials play a role in the success of your program? What is at risk when leaders do not have the necessary competencies and qualities of leadership essentials necessary for leading people?

Next Steps

This book contains many strategies and activities to help you embed the Whole Leadership Framework in your work as a leader. Where will you begin? List three action steps.

_____

_____

_____

_____

_____

_____

References and Recommended Reading

Chapter 1

Abel, Mike, Teri Talan, and Marie Masterson. 2017. "Whole Leadership: A Framework for Early Childhood Programs." *Exchange* 39(233): 22–25.

Ammer, Christine. 2003. "Influence." *The American Heritage Dictionary of Idioms*. Boston, MA: Houghton Mifflin.

Ang, Lynn. 2012. "Leading and Managing in the Early Years: A Study of the Impact of a NCSL Programme on Children's Center Leader's Perceptions of Leadership and Practice." *Educational Management Administration and Leadership* 40(3): 289–304.

Bloom, Paula Jorde. 2014. *Leadership in Action: How Effective Leaders Get Things Done*. Lake Forest, IL: New Horizons.

Camilli, Gregory, Sadako Vargas, Sharon Ryan, and W. Steven Barnett. 2010. "Meta-Analysis of the Effects of Early Education Interventions on Cognitive and Social Development." *Teachers College Record* 112(3): 579–620.

Carter, Margie. 2016. "Leadership Challenges in Publicly Funded Preschools." *Exchange* 228(March/April): 26–31.

Centers for Disease Control and Prevention (CDC). 2018. "Whole School, Whole Community, Whole Child (WSCC)." CDC. https://www.cdc.gov/healthyschools/wscc/index.htm

Coleman, Andy, Caroline Sharp, and Graham Handscomb. 2016. "Leading Highly Performing Children's Centres: Supporting the Development of the 'Accidental Leaders.'" *Educational Management Administration and Leadership* 44(5): 775–793.

Colmer, Kaye, Manjula Waniganayake, and Laurie Field. 2014. "Leading Professional Learning in Early Childhood Centres: Who Are the Educational Leaders?" *Australasian Journal of Early Childhood* 39(4): 103–113.

Dennis, Sarah, and Erin O'Connor. 2013. "Reexamining Quality in Early Childhood Education: Exploring the Relationship between the Organizational Climate and the Classroom." *Journal of Research in Childhood Education* 27(1): 74–92.

Derman-Sparks, Louise, John Nimmo, and Debbie LeeKeenan. 2015. "Leadership Matters: Creating Anti-Bias Change in Early Childhood Programs." *Exchange* 226(November/December): 8–11.

Early Childhood Systems Working Group (ECSWG). 2014. "Comprehensive Early Childhood System-Building: A Tool to Inform Discussions on Collaborative, Cross-Sector Planning." http://www.buildinitiative.org/Portals/0/Uploads/Documents/ECSWG%20Systems%20Planning%20Tool_2014.pdf

Fuller, Bruce, John Gasko, and Rebecca Anguiano. 2012. "Lifting Preschool Quality: Nurturing Effective Teachers." In *Handbook of Research on the Education of Young Children*. London, UK: Routledge.

Hay, Susan. 2012. "Maturing as a Manager: Bringing Leadership and Management Together." *Exchange* 203(January/February): 12–14.

Kuhl, Patricia K. 2011. "Early Language Learning and Literacy: Neuroscience Implications for Education." *Mind, Brain, and Education* 5(3): 128–142.

Lieberman, Abbie. 2017. "A Tale of Two Pre-K Leaders: How State Policies for Center Directors and Principals Leading Pre-K Programs Differ, and Why They Shouldn't." Policy Paper. Washington, DC: New America.

Masterson, Marie L. 2018. *Let's Talk Toddlers: A Practical Guide to High-Quality Teaching*. St. Paul, MN: Redleaf.

Minkos, Marlena, et al. 2017. "Culturally Responsive Practice and the Role of School Administrators." *Psychology in the Schools* 54(10): 1260–1266.

Nuttall, Joce, Louise Thomas, and Linda Henderson. 2018. "Formative Interventions in Leadership Development in Early Childhood Education: The Potential of Double Stimulation." *Journal of Early Childhood Research* 16(1): 80–91.

Ostroff, Cheri, Angelo Kinicki, and Rabiah Muhammad. 2013. "Organizational Culture and Climate." In *Handbook of Psychology*. 2nd ed. Hoboken, NJ: John Wiley and Sons.

Talan, Teri, Paula Jorde Bloom, and Robyn Kelton. 2014. "Building the Leadership Capacity of Early Childhood Directors: An Evaluation of a Leadership Development Model." *Early Childhood Research and Practice* 16(1 and 2): n.p. http://ecrp.uiuc.edu/v16n1/talan.html

Tout, Kathryn, Dale Epstein, Meg Soli, and Claire Lowe. 2015. "A Blueprint for Early Care and Education Quality Improvement Initiatives: Final Report." Child Trends. https://www.childtrends.org/wp-content/uploads/2015/03/2015-07BlueprintEarlyCareandEd.pdf

Weldon, Arianne. 2014. "Language Nutrition: Filling the Word Opportunity Gap." Speech presented at the National Meeting of State Leads for the National Campaign for Grade-Level Reading, Washington, DC, January 9.

Zauche, Lauren Head, Taylor A. Thul, Ashley E. Darcy Mahoney, and Jennifer L. Stapel-Wax. 2016. "Influence of Language Nutrition on Children's Language and Cognitive Development: An Integrated Review." *Early Childhood Research Quarterly* 36(3rd q.): 318–333.

Chapter 2

Bandura, Albert. 1986. *Social Foundations of Thought and Action: A Social-Cognitive Theory* Englewood Cliffs, NJ: Prentice-Hall.

Bandura, Albert. 1993. "Perceived Self-Efficacy in Cognitive Development and Functioning." *Educational Psychologist* 28(2): 117–148.

Bandura, Albert. 1997. *Self-Efficacy: The Exercise of Control*. New York, NY: W. H. Freeman.

Batey, Mark. 2011. "Is Creativity the Number 1 Skill for the 21st Century?" *Psychology Today*. https://www.psychologytoday.com/us/blog/working-creativity/201102/is-creativity-the-number-1-skill-the-21st-century

Bruno, Holly Elissa, Janet Gonzalez-Mena, Luis Hernandez, and Debra Sullivan. 2015. "Leading with Humor and Humility." *Exchange* 228(November/December): 55–58.

Caldwell, Cam, Riki Ichiho, and Verl Anderson. 2017. "Understanding Level 5 Leaders: The Ethical Perspectives of Leadership Humility." *Journal of Management Development* 36(5): 724–732.

Çalik, Temel, Ferudun Sezgin, Hasan Kavgaci, and Ali Çağatay Kilinc. 2012. "Examination of Relationships between Instructional Leadership of School Principals and Self-Efficacy of Teachers and Collective Teacher Efficacy." *Educational Sciences: Theory and Practice* 12(4): 2498–2504.

Denham, Susanne, Hideko Bassett, and Susanne Miller. 2017. "Early Childhood Teachers' Socialization of Emotion: Contextual and Individual Contributors." *Child Youth Care Forum* 46(6): 805–824.

Donohoo, Jenni. 2018. "Collective Teacher Efficacy Research: Productive Patterns of Behavior and Other Positive Consequences." *Journal of Educational Change* 19(3): 323–345.

Donohoo, Jenni, John Hattie, and Rachel Eells. 2018. "The Power of Collective Efficacy." *Educational Leadership* 75(6): 40–44.

Duignan, Patrick. 2014. "Authenticity in Educational Leadership: History, Ideal, Reality." *Journal of Educational Administration* 52(2): 152–172.

Dunkley, Chad. 2017. "Growing a Multi-Site Organization." *Exchange* 39(January/February): 18–20.

Dweck, Carol S. 2016. *Mindset: The New Psychology of Success*. New York, NY: Ballantine.

Eklund, Jakob, Teresia Andersson-Stråberg, and Eric M. Hansen. 2009. "'I've Also Experienced Loss and Fear': Effects of Prior Similar Experience on Empathy." *Scandinavian Journal of Psychology* 50(1): 65–69.

Frederick, Heidi, James Wood Jr., George West, and Bruce Winston. 2016. "The Effect of the Accountability Variables of Responsibility, Openness, and Answerability on Authentic Leadership." *Journal of Research on Christian Education* 25(3): 302–316.

Guilmartin, Nance. 2010. "Giving One Pause: Learn How Cultivating Humility Can Drive Success, Even in the Most Time-, Budget-, and Attention-Stressed Workplaces." *Talent Development* 64(3): 72–73.

Hannah, Sean, Fred Walumbwa, and Louis Fry. 2011. "Leadership in Action Teams: Team Leader and Members' Authenticity, Authenticity Strength, and Team Outcomes." *Personnel Psychology* 64(3): 771–802.

Jeon, Lieny, Cynthia Buettner, and Ashley Grant. 2018. "Early Childhood Teachers' Psychological Well-Being: Exploring Potential Predictors of Depression, Stress, and Emotional Exhaustion." *Early Education and Development* 29(1): 53–69.

Jiang, Hua, and Rita Linjuan Men. 2017. "Creating an Engaged Workforce: The Impact of Authentic Leadership, Transparent Organizational Communication, and Work-Life Enrichment." *Communication Research* 44(2): 225–243.

Kelleher, Joanne. 2016. "You're OK, I'm OK." *Phi Delta Kappan* 97(8): 70–73.

Marshall, Liam E., and William L. Marshall. 2011. "Empathy and Antisocial Behaviour." *Journal of Forensic Psychiatry and Psychology* 22(5): 742–759.

Masterson, Marie, and Katharine Kersey. 2013 "Connecting Children to Kindness: Encouraging a Culture of Empathy." *Childhood Education* 89(4): 211–216.

McCormick, Michael, Jesús Tanguma, and Anita Sohn López-Forment. 2002. "Extending Self-Efficacy Theory to Leadership: A Review and Empirical Test." *Journal of Leadership Education* 1(2): 34–49.

Muñoz, Martha, Pam Boulton, Tamara Johnson, and Cigdem Unal. 2015. "Leadership Development for a Changing Early Childhood Landscape." *Young Children* 70(2): 26–31.

Owens, Bradley. 2009. "The Utility of Humility in Organizations: Establishing Construct, Nomological, and Predictive Validity." *Academy of Management Proceedings* 2009(1): 1–6.

Oyer, Brenda. 2015. "Teacher Perceptions of Principals' Confidence, Humility, and Effectiveness." *Journal of School Leadership* 25(4): 684–719.

Pavlovich, Kathryn, and Keiko Krahnke. 2011. "Empathy, Connectedness and Organization." *Journal of Business Ethics* 105(1): 131–137.

Polychroniou, Panagiotis V. 2009. "Relationship between Emotional Intelligence and Transformational Leadership of Supervisors: The Impact on Team Effectiveness." *Team Performance Management* 15(7/8): 343–356.

Ryan, Richard, and Edward Deci. 2013. "Toward a Social Psychology of Assimilation: Self-Determination Theory in Cognitive Development and Education." In *Self-Regulation and Autonomy: Social and Developmental Dimensions of Human Conduct*. Cambridge, UK: Cambridge University.

Stoll, Louise, and Julie Temperley. 2009. "Creative Leadership Teams: Capacity Building and Succession Planning." *Management in Education* 23(1): 12–18.

Tomlinson, Carol Ann, and Michael Murphy. 2018. "The Empathetic School." *Educational Leadership* 75(6): 20–27.

Tschannen-Moran, Megan, and Bob Tschannen-Moran. 2014. "What to Do When Your School's in a Bad Mood." *Educational Leadership* 71(5): 36–41.

Walumbwa, Fred, et al. 2008. "Authentic Leadership: Development and Validation of a Theory-Based Measure." *Journal of Management* 34(1): 89–126.

Warren, Rick. 2002. *The Purpose-Driven Life: What on Earth Am I Here For?* Grand Rapids, MI: Zondervan.

Wasonga, Teresa. 2010. "Co-Creating Leadership Dispositional Values and Contexts Survey." *International Journal of Educational Management* 24(3): 266–278.

Wells, Michael B. 2015. "Predicting Preschool Teacher Retention and Turnover in Newly Hired Head Start Teachers across the First Half of the School Year." *Early Childhood Research Quarterly* 30A(1): 152–159.

Wexler, Bruce. 2008. *Brain and Culture: Neurobiology, Ideology, and Social Change*. Cambridge, MA: The MIT Press.

Chapter 3

Aas, Marit. 2017. "Leaders as Learners: Developing New Leadership Practices." *Professional Development in Education* 43(3): 439–453.

Bella, Jill. 2016. *A Critical Intersection: Administrative and Pedagogical Leadership*. Wheeling, IL: McCormick Center for Early Childhood Leadership. https://mccormick-assets.floodlight.design/wp-content/uploads/2018/03/4-18-16_ACriticalIntersection-AdministrativeAndPedagogical Leadership.pdf

Bloom, Paula Jorde, and Michael Abel. 2015. "Expanding the Lens: Leadership as an Organizational Asset." *Young Children* 70(2). https://www.naeyc.org/resources/pubs/yc/may2015/expanding-the-lens

Bloom, Paula Jorde, Ann Hentschel, and Jill Bella. 2013. *Inspiring Peak Performance: Competence, Commitment, and Collaboration*. Lake Forest, IL: New Horizons.

Cameron, Kim. 2011. "Responsible Leadership as Virtuous Leadership." *Journal of Business Ethics* 98(Supp. 1): 25–35.

Chen, Dora, John Nimmo, and Heather Fraser. 2009. "Becoming a Culturally Responsive Early Childhood Educator: A Tool to Support Reflection by Teachers Embarking on the Anti-Bias Journey." *Multicultural Perspectives* 11(2): 101–106.

Feeney, Stephanie. 2010. "Ethics Today in Early Care and Education: Review, Reflection, and the Future." *Young Children* 65(2): 72–77.

Goleman, Daniel, Richard Boyatzis, and Annie McKee. 2013. *Primal Leadership: Unleashing the Power of Emotional Intelligence.* Boston, MA: Harvard Business Review Press.

Halgunseth, Linda, Gisela Jia, and Oscar Barbarin. 2013. "Family Engagement in Early Childhood Programs: Serving Families of Dual Language Learners." In *California's Best Practices for Young Dual Language Learners.* Sacramento, CA: California Department of Education.

Hinkle, Robin. 2018. "Increasing Student Self-Awareness to Prepare Tomorrow's Leaders." *International Journal of Education Research* 13(1): 42–54.

Johnson, Lauri, and Carrie Fuller. 2015. "Culturally Responsive Leadership." In *Oxford Bibliographies in Education.* New York, NY: Oxford University Press.

Khalifa, Muhammad, Mark Gooden, and James Davis. 2016. "Culturally Responsive School Leadership: A Synthesis of the Literature." *Review of Educational Research* 86(4): 1272–1311.

NAEYC. 2006/2011. *NAEYC Code of Ethical Conduct: Supplement for Early Childhood Program Administrators.* Washington, DC: NAEYC.

NAEYC. 2011. *Code of Ethical Conduct and Statement of Commitment.* https://www.naeyc.org/files/naeyc/file/positions/PSETH05.pdf

Nevarez, Michele. 2017. "In Focus: Self-Awareness Is the Gateway for Developing Positive Leadership Capacity." *Talent Development* 71(3): 54–58.

Nicholson, Julie, and Helen Maniates. 2015. "Recognizing Postmodern Intersectional Identities in Leadership for Early Childhood." *Early Years: Journal of International Research and Development* 36(1): 66–80.

O'Gorman, Lyndal, and Louise Hard. 2013. "Looking Back and Looking Forward: Exploring Distributed Leadership with Queensland Prep Teachers." *Australasian Journal of Early Childhood* 38(3): 77–84.

Pianta, Robert. 2012. "Taking Seriously the Needs and Capacity of the Early Childhood Care and Education Workforce." *Social Policy Report* 26(1): 27–28.

Pink, Daniel H. 2009. *Drive: The Surprising Truth about What Motivates Us.* New York, NY: Riverhead.

Ruprecht, Karen, James Elicker, and Ji Young Choi. 2016. "Continuity of Care, Caregiver-Child Interactions, and Toddler Social Competence and Problem Behaviors." *Early Education and Development* 27(2): 221–239.

Ryan, Sharon, Marcy Whitebook, Fran Kipnis, and Laura Sakai. 2011. "Professional Development Needs of Directors Leading in a Mixed Service Delivery Preschool System." *Early Childhood Research and Practice* 13(1): n.p. http://ecrp.uiuc.edu/v13n1/ryan.html

Santamaría, Lorri J. 2013. "Critical Change for the Greater Good: Multicultural Perceptions in Educational Leadership toward Social Justice and Equity." *Educational Administration Quarterly* 50(3): 347–391.

Schulman, Karen, Hannah Matthews, Helen Blank, and Danielle Ewen. 2012. *A Count for Quality: Childcare Center Directors on Rating and Improvement Systems.* Washington, DC: National Women's Law Center and Center for Law and Social Policy (CLASP). https://files.eric.ed.gov/fulltext/ED538044.pdf

Sims, Margaret, Rhonda Forrest, Anthony Semann, and Colin Slattery. 2015. "Conceptions of Early Childhood Leadership: Driving New Professionalism?" *International Journal of Leadership in Education* 18(2): 149–166.

Stamopoulos, Elizabeth. 2012. "Reframing Early Childhood Leadership." *Australasian Journal of Early Childhood* 37(2): 42–48.

Wright, Nicholas Thomas. 2010. *Virtue Reborn*. New York, NY: HarperCollins.

Zinsser, Katherine, Susanne Denham, Timothy Curby, and Rachel Chazan-Cohen. 2016. "Early Childhood Directors as Socializers of Emotional Climate." *Learning Environment Research* 19(2): 267–290.

Chapter 4

Abel, Michael, Teri Talan, Kelly Pollitt, and Laura Bornfreund. 2016. "National Principals' Survey on Early Childhood Instructional Leadership." Wheeling, IL: McCormick Center for Early Childhood Leadership Publications. http://digitalcommons.nl.edu/mccormickcenter-pubs/1

Barrueco, Sandra, Sheila Smith, and Samuel Stephens. 2015. *Supporting Parent Engagement in Linguistically Diverse Families to Promote Young Children's Learning: Implications for Early Care and Education Policy*. New York, NY: Child Care and Early Education Research Connections. https://www.researchconnections.org/childcare/resources/30185/pdf

Berk, Laura, and Adam Winsler. 1995. *Scaffolding Children's Learning: Vygotsky and Early Childhood Education*. NAEYC Research into Practice Series, volume 7. Washington, DC: NAEYC.

Bodrova, Elena, and Deborah Leong. 2007. *Tools of the Mind: The Vygotskian Approach to Early Childhood Education*. 2nd ed. Upper Saddle River, NJ: Pearson.

Bodrova, Elena, Deborah Leong, and Tatiana Akhutina. 2011. "When Everything New Is Well-Forgotten Old: Vygotsky/Luria Insights in the Development of Executive Functions." *New Directions for Child and Adolescent Development* 2019(33): 11–28.

Bowes, Lucy, et al. 2013. "Chronic Bullying Victimization across School Transitions: The Role of Genetic and Environmental Influences." *Development and Psychopathology* 25(2): 333–346.

Cole, Sylvia. 2017. "The Impact of Parental Involvement on Academic Achievement." Doctoral diss. San Diego, CA: Northcentral University.

Daly, Alan, et al. 2014. "The Rise of Neurotics: Social Networks, Leadership, and Efficacy in District Reform." *Educational Administration Quarterly* 50(2): 233–278.

Diamond, John, and James Spillane. 2016. "School Leadership and Management from a Distributed Perspective: A 2016 Retrospective and Prospective." *Management in Education* 30(4): 147–154.

Dombro, Amy Laura, Charlotte Stetson, and Judy Jablon. 2011. *Powerful Interactions: How to Connect with Children to Extend their Learning*. Washington, DC: NAEYC.

Early Math Collaborative, Erikson Institute. 2013. *Big Ideas of Early Mathematics: What Teachers of Young Children Need to Know*. Boston, MA: Pearson.

Edwards, Carolyn, Lella Gandini, and George Forman, eds. 1993. *The Hundred Languages of Children: The Reggio Emilia Approach to Early Childhood Education*. Norwood, NJ: Ablex.

Epstein, Ann. 2007. *The Intentional Teacher: Choosing the Best Strategies for Young Children's Learning*. Washington, DC: NAEYC.

Forry, Nicole, et al. 2012. "Family-Provider Relationship Quality Measurement Development Project: Review of Conceptual and Empirical Literature of Family-Provider Relationships." *OPRE Report #2012-46*. Washington, DC: Office of Planning, Research, and Evaluation, Administration for Children and Families, U.S. Department of Health and Human Services. https://www.acf.hhs.gov/sites/default/files/opre/fprq_literature_review.pdf

Graves, Scott Jr., and Lynda Brown Wright. 2011. "Parent Involvement at School Entry: A National Examination of Group Differences and Achievement." *School Psychology International* 32(1): 35–48.

Harrison, Cindy, and Joellen Killion. 2007. "Ten Roles for Teacher Leaders." *Educational Leadership* 65(1): 74–77.

Hassinger-Das, Brenna, Kathy Hirsh-Pasek, and Roberta Michnick Golinkoff. 2017. "The Case of Brain Science and Guided Play: A Developing Story." *Young Children* 72(2): 45.

Henderson, Anne, and Karen Mapp. 2002. *A New Wave of Evidence: The Impact of School, Family, and Community Connections on Student Achievement*. Austin, TX: National Center for Family and Community Connections with Schools, Southwest Educational Development Laboratory. https://www.sedl.org/connections/resources/evidence.pdf

Kersey, Katharine, and Marie Masterson. 2012. *101 Principals for Positive Guidance with Young Children: Creating Responsive Teachers*. Boston, MA: Pearson.

Kim, Elizabeth Moorman, et al. 2012. "Parent Involvement and Family-School Partnerships: Examining the Content, Processes, and Outcomes of Structural versus Relationship-Based Approaches." *CYFS Working Paper No. 2012-6*. Lincoln, NE: Nebraska Center for Research on Children, Youth, Families, and Schools. https://files.eric.ed.gov/fulltext/ED537851.pdf

Mashburn, Andrew, Laura Justice, Jason Downer, and Robert Pianta. 2009. "Peer Effects on Children's Language Achievement during Pre-Kindergarten." *Child Development* (May/June) 80(3): 686–702.

Masterson, Marie L. 2018. *Let's Talk Toddlers: A Practical Guide to High-Quality Teaching*. St. Paul, MN: Redleaf.

Masterson, Marie, and Katharine Kersey. 2016. *Enjoying the Parenting Roller Coaster: Nurturing and Empowering Your Children Through the Ups and Downs*. Lewisville, NC: Gryphon House.

McCormick, Meghan, Elise Cappella, Erin O'Connor, and Sandee McClowry. 2015. "Social-Emotional Learning and Academic Achievement: Using Causal Methods to Explore Classroom-Level Mechanisms." *AERA Open* 1(3): 1–26.

McCrory, Eamon, Stephane A. De Brito, and Essi Viding. 2010. "Research Review: The Neurobiology and Genetics of Maltreatment and Adversity." *Journal of Child Psychology and Psychiatry* 51(10): 1079–1095.

Mokrova, Irina, et al. 2013. "The Role of Persistence at Preschool Age in Academic Skills at Kindergarten." *European Journal of Psychology of Education* 28(4): 1495–1503.

NAEYC. 2018. *NAEYC Early Learning Program Accreditation Standards and Assessment Items*. Washington, DC: NAEYC. https://www.naeyc.org/sites/default/files/globally-shared/downloads/PDFs/accreditation/early-learning/standards_and_assessment_web_1.pdf

Powell, Douglas, Seung-Hee Son, Nancy File, and Robert San Juan. 2010. "Parent-School Relationships and Children's Academic and Social Outcomes in Public School Pre-Kindergarten." *Journal of School Psychology* 48(4): 269–292.

Rikoon, Samuel, Paul McDermott, and John Fantuzzo. 2012. "Approaches to Learning among Head Start Alumni: Structure and Validity of the Learning Behaviors Scale." *School Psychology Review* 41(3): 272–294.

Roggman, Lori, Lisa Boyce, and Gina Cook. 2009. "Keeping Kids on Track: Impacts of a Parenting-Focused Early Head Start Program on Attachment Security and Cognitive Development." *Early Education and Development* 20(6): 920–941.

Snow, Catherine, and Susan Van Hemel, eds. 2008. *Early Childhood Assessment: Why, What, and How.* Washington, DC: The National Academies Press.

Strasser, Janis, and Lisa M. Bresson. 2017. *Big Questions for Young Minds: Extending Children's Thinking.* Washington, DC: NAEYC.

Vygotsky, Lev S. 1978. *Mind in Society: The Development of Higher Psychological Processes.* Cambridge, MA: Harvard University Press.

Wilder, Sandra. 2014. "Effects of Parental Involvement on Academic Achievement: A Meta-Synthesis." *Educational Review* 66(3): 377–397.

Williford, Amanda, Jessica Vick Whittaker, Virginia Vitiello, and Jason Downer. 2013. "Children's Engagement within the Preschool Classroom and Their Development of Self-Regulation." *Early Education Development* 24(2): 162–187.

Chapter 5

Booren, Leslie, Jason Downer, and Virginia Vitiello. 2012. "Observations of Children's Interactions with Teachers, Peers, and Tasks across Preschool Classroom Activity Settings." *Early Education and Development* 23(4): 515–538.

Buettner, Cynthia, Lieny Jeon, Eunhye Hur, and Rachel Garcia. 2016. "Teachers' Social-Emotional Capacity: Factors Associated with Teachers' Responsiveness and Professional Commitment." *Early Education and Development* 27(7): 1018–1039.

Chien, Nina, et al. 2010. "Children's Classroom Engagement and School Readiness Gains in Prekindergarten." *Child Development* 81(5): 1534–1549.

Commodari, Elena. 2013. "Preschool Teacher Attachment, School Readiness, and Risk of Learning Difficulties." *Early Childhood Research Quarterly* 28(1): 123–133.

Conn-Powers, Michael. 2013. "Teacher-Child Interactions That Make a Difference." *Early Childhood Center.* https://www.iidc.indiana.edu/styles/iidc/defiles/ecc/ecc_teacherchildinteractions_time_curriculum.pdf

De Franchis, Valentina, Maria Carmen Usai, Paola Viterbori, and Laura Traverso. 2017. "Preschool Executive Functioning and Literacy Achievement in Grades 1 and 3 of Primary School: A Longitudinal Study." *Learning and Individual Differences* 54: 184–195.

Denham, Susanne, et al. 2013. "Social and Emotional Information Processing in Preschoolers: Indicator of Early School Success?" *Early Child Development and Care* 183(5): 667–688.

Derman-Sparks, Louise, Debbie LeeKeenan, and John Nimmo. 2015. *Leading Anti-Bias Early Childhood Programs: A Guide for Change.* New York, NY: Teachers College Press.

Dombro, Amy Laura, Charlotte Stetson, and Judy Jablon. 2011. *Powerful Interactions: How to Connect with Children to Extend their Learning.* Washington, DC: NAEYC.

Espinosa, Linda M. 2005. "Curriculum and Assessment Considerations for Young Children from Culturally, Linguistically, and Economically Diverse Backgrounds." *Psychology in the Schools* 42(8): 837–853.

Fitzpatrick, Caroline, and Linda Pagani. 2011. "Toddler Working Memory Skills Predict Kindergarten School Readiness." *Intelligence* 40(2): 205–212.

Fixsen, Dean, et al. 2005. *A Review and Synthesis of the Literature Related to the Implementation of Programs and Practices*. Tampa, FL: University of South Florida, Louise de la Parte Florida Mental Health Institute, The National Implementation Research Network. https://nirn.fpg.unc.edu/sites/nirn.fpg.unc.edu/files/resources/NIRN-MonographFull-01-2005.pdf

Gillanders, Cristina, Dina Castro, and Ximena Franco. 2014. "Learning Words for Life: Promoting Vocabulary in Dual Language Learners." *The Reading Teacher* 68(3): 213–221.

Goble, Priscilla, et al. 2016. "Preschool Contexts and Teacher Interactions: Relations with School Readiness." *Early Education and Development* 27(5): 623–641.

Goble, Priscilla, and Robert C. Pianta. 2017. "Teacher-Child Interactions in Free Choice and Teacher-Directed Activity Settings: Prediction to School Readiness." *Early Education and Development* 28(8): 1035–1051.

Goldstein, Howard, and Arnold Olszewski. 2015. "Developing a Phonological Awareness Curriculum: Reflections on an Implementation Science Framework." *Journal of Speech, Language, and Hearing Research* 58(6): S1837–S1850.

Hall-Kenyon, Kendra, Robert Bullough, Kathryn Lake Mackay, and Esther Marshall. 2014. "Preschool Teacher Well-Being: A Review of the Literature." *Early Childhood Education Journal* 42(3): 153–162.

Hirsh-Pasek, Kathy, et al. 2015. "Putting Education in 'Educational' Apps: Lessons from the Science of Learning." *Psychological Science in the Public Interest* 16(1): 3–24.

Isik-Ercan, Zeynep, and Kelley Perkins. 2017. "Reflection for Meaning and Action as an Engine for Professional Development across Multiple Early Childhood Teacher-Education Contexts." *Journal of Early Childhood Teacher Education* 38(4): 342–354.

Jennings, Patricia, et al. 2014. "Impacts of the CARE for Teachers Program on Teachers' Social and Emotional Competence and Classroom Interactions." *Journal of Educational Psychology* 109(7): 1010–1028.

Jeon, Lieny, Cynthia Buettner, and Ashley Grant. 2018. "Early Childhood Teachers' Psychological Well-Being: Exploring Potential Predictors of Depression, Stress, and Emotional Exhaustion." *Early Education and Development* 29(1): 53–69.

Jeon, Lieny, Cynthia Buettner, and Eunhye Hur. 2016. "Preschool Teachers' Professional Background, Process Quality, and Job Attitudes: A Person-Centered Approach." *Early Education and Development* 27(4): 551–571.

Knowles, Malcolm S. 1984. *Andragogy in Action: Applying Modern Principles of Adult Learning*. San Francisco, CA: Jossey-Bass.

Kuh, Lisa, et al. 2016. "Moving Beyond Anti-Bias Activities: Supporting the Development of Anti-Bias Practices." *Young Children* 71(1): 58–65.

Luna, Sara Michael. 2017. "Academic Language in Preschool: Research and Context." *The Reading Teacher* 71(1): 89–93.

Mashburn, Andrew, et al. 2008. "Measures of Classroom Quality in Prekindergarten and Children's Development of Academic, Language, and Social Skills." *Child Development* 79(3): 732–749.

Massing, Christine, Anna Kirova, and Kelly Hennig. 2013. "The Role of First-Language Facilitators in Redefining Parent Involvement: Newcomer Families' Funds of Knowledge in an Intercultural Preschool Program." *Journal of Childhood Studies* 38(2): 4–13.

NAEYC. 2018. *NAEYC Early Learning Program Accreditation Standards and Assessment Items*. Washington, DC: NAEYC. https://www.naeyc.org/sites/default/files/globally-shared/downloads/PDFs/accreditation/early-learning/standards_and_assessment_web_1.pdf

Phillion, JoAnn. 2002. *Narrative Inquiry in a Multicultural Landscape: Multicultural Teaching and Learning*. Westport, CT: Ablex.

Purper, Cammy. 2016. "Right at Your Fingertips: Important Web-Based Resources for Understanding Evidence-Based Practices." *Early Childhood Education Journal* 44(4): 403–408.

Thomason, Amy, and Karen La Paro. 2013. "Teachers' Commitment to the Field and Teacher-Child Interactions in Center-Based Child Care for Toddlers and Three Year-Olds." *Early Childhood Education Journal* 41(3): 227–234.

Whittaker, Jessica Vick, and Mary Benson McMullen. 2014. "Good Thinking! Fostering Children's Reasoning and Problem Solving." *Young Children* 69(3): 80–89.

Chapter 6

Ancell, Katherine, Deborah A. Bruns, and Jonathan Chitiyo. 2018. "The Importance of Father Involvement in Early Childhood Programs." *Young Exceptional Children* 21(1): 22–23.

Baker, Megina. 2019. "Playing, Talking, Co-Constructing: Exemplary Teaching for Young Dual Language Learners across Program Types." *Early Childhood Education Journal* 47(1): 115–130.

Bartlett, Jessica, Sheila Smith, and Elizabeth Bringewatt. 2017. *Helping Young Children Who Have Experienced Trauma: Policies and Strategies for Early Care and Education*. Child Trends Report. New York, NY: National Center for Children in Poverty, Columbia University, Mailman School of Public Health. https://www.childtrends.org/wp-content/uploads/2017/04/2017-19ECETrauma.pdf

Bella, Jill. 2016. *A Critical Intersection: Administrative and Pedagogical Leadership*. Wheeling, IL: McCormick Center for Early Childhood Leadership. https://mccormick-assets.floodlight.design/wp-content/uploads/2018/03/4-18-16_ACriticalIntersection-AdministrativeAndPedagogicalLeadership.pdf

Christenson, Sandra, and Amy Reschly, eds. 2010. *Handbook of School-Family Partnerships*. New York, NY: Routledge.

DeSocio, Janiece. 2015. "A Call to Action: Reducing Toxic Stress during Pregnancy and Early Childhood." *Journal of Child and Adolescent Psychiatric Nursing* 28(2): 70–71.

Djonko-Moore, Cara, and Linda Traum. 2015. "The Influence of Early Childhood Educators' Teacher Preparation and Efficacy on Culturally Responsive Teaching Practices." *Teacher Education and Practice* 28(1): 156–176.

Dinehart, Laura, Lynne Katz, Louis Manfra, and Mary Anne Ullery. 2013. "Providing Quality Early Care and Education to Young Children Who Experience Maltreatment: A Review of the Literature." *Early Childhood Education Journal* 41(4): 283–290.

Epstein, Joyce. 2001. *School, Family, and Community Partnerships: Preparing Educators and Improving Schools*. Boulder, CO: Westview.

Fort, Pilar, and Robert Stechuk. 2008. "The Cultural Responsiveness and Dual Language Education Project." *Zero to Three* 29(1): 24–28.

Friedman-Krauss, Allison, C. Cybele Raver, Juliana Neuspiel, and John Kinsel. 2014. "Child Behavior Problems, Teacher Executive Functions, and Teacher Stress in Head Start Classrooms." *Early Education and Development* 25(5): 681–702.

Gillanders, Cristina, Dina Castro, and Ximena Franco. 2014. "Learning Words for Life: Promoting Vocabulary in Dual Language Learners." *The Reading Teacher* 68(3): 213–221.

Halgunseth, Linda. 2009. "Family Engagement, Diverse Families, and Early Childhood Education Programs: An Integrated Review of the Literature." *Young Children* 64(5): 56–58.

Hatfield, Bridget, Linda Hestenes, Victoria Kintner-Duffy, and Marion O'Brien. 2013. "Classroom Emotional Support Predicts Differences in Preschool Children's Cortisol and Alpha-Amylase Levels." *Early Childhood Research Quarterly* 28(2): 347–356.

Holmes, Cheryl, et al. 2015 "A Model for Creating a Supportive Trauma-Informed Culture for Children in Preschool Settings." *Journal of Child and Family Studies* 24(6): 1650–1659.

Institute of Medicine and National Research Council. 2015. *Transforming the Workforce for Children Birth through Age 8: A Unifying Foundation*. Washington, DC: The National Academies Press. https://www.fcd-us.org/assets/2016/10/IOMNRCFullReport2015.pdf

Kersey, Katharine, and Marie Masterson. 2009. "Teachers Connecting with Families—In the Best Interest of Children." *Young Children* 64(5): 34–38.

Ladson-Billings, Gloria. 1995. "Toward a Theory of Culturally Relevant Pedagogy." *American Educational Research Journal* 32(3): 465–491.

Lang, Sarah, Angela Tolbert, Sarah Schoppe-Sullivan, and Amy Bonomi. 2016. "A Cocaring Framework for Infants and Toddlers: Applying a Model of Coparenting to Parent-Teacher Relationships." *Early Childhood Research Quarterly* 34(1): 40–52.

Larocque, Michelle, Ira Kleiman, and Sharon Darling. 2011. "Parental Involvement: The Missing Link in School Achievement." *Preventing School Failure* 55(3): 115–122.

Lipina, Sebastián. 2016. "The Biological Side of Social Determinants: Neural Costs of Childhood Poverty." *Prospects* 46(2): 265–280.

Longstreth, Sascha, et al. 2016. "Teacher Perspectives on the Practice of Continuity of Care." *Journal of Research in Childhood Education* 30(4): 554–568.

Masterson, Marie L. 2018. *Let's Talk Toddlers: A Practical Guide to High-Quality Teaching*. St. Paul, MN: Redleaf.

McCrory, Eamon, Stephane A. De Brito, and Essi Viding. 2010. "Research Review: The Neurobiology and Genetics of Maltreatment and Adversity." *Journal of Child Psychology and Psychiatry* 51(10): 1079–1095.

Modica, Sarah, Maya Ajmera, and Victoria Dunning. 2010. "Meeting Children Where They Are: Culturally Adapted Models of Early Childhood Education." *Young Children* 65(6): 20–26.

Mortensen, Jennifer, and Melissa Barnett. 2016. "The Role of Child Care in Supporting the Emotion Regulatory Needs of Maltreated Infants and Toddlers." *Children and Youth Services Review* 64: 73–81.

NAEYC. 2009. "Quality Benchmark for Cultural Competence Project." https://www.naeyc.org/sites/default/files/globally-shared/downloads/PDFs/our-work/public-policy-advocacy/QBCC_Tool%20%281%29.pdf

National Center for Children in Poverty. 2018. "Young Child Risk Calculator." National Center for Children in Poverty, Columbia University, Mailman School of Public Health. http://www.nccp.org/tools/risk/

National Child Traumatic Stress Network. 2018. "Creating Trauma-Informed Systems." National Child Traumatic Stress Network. https://www.nctsn.org/trauma-informed-care/creating-trauma-informed-systems

National Scientific Council on the Developing Child. 2005/2014. *Excessive Stress Disrupts the Architecture of the Developing Brain: Working Paper 3*. Updated ed. Cambridge, MA: National Scientific Council on the Developing Child, Center on the Developing Child at Harvard University. https://46y5eh11fhgw3ve3ytpwxt9r-wpengine.netdna-ssl.com/wp-content/uploads/2005/05/Stress_Disrupts_Architecture_Developing_Brain-1.pdf

National Scientific Council on the Developing Child. 2010. *Persistent Fear and Anxiety Can Affect Young Children's Learning and Development: Working Paper No. 9*. Cambridge, MA: National Scientific Council on the Developing Child, Center on the Developing Child at Harvard University. https://46y5eh11fhgw3ve3ytpwxt9r-wpengine.netdna-ssl.com/wp-content/uploads/2010/05/Persistent-Fear-and-Anxiety-Can-Affect-Young-Childrens-Learning-and-Development.pdf

Nitecki, Elena. 2015. "Integrated School-Family Partnerships in Preschool: Building Quality Involvement through Multidimensional Relationships." *School Community Journal* 25(2): 195–219.

Park, Maki, Anna O'Toole, and Caitlin Katsiaficas. 2017. *Dual Language Learners: A National Demographic and Policy Profile*. Washington, DC: Migration Policy Institute, National Center on Immigration Integration Policy. https://www.migrationpolicy.org/research/dual-language-learners-national-demographic-and-policy-profile

Phillips, Deborah, Lea Austin, and Marcy Whitebook. 2016. "The Early Care and Education Workforce." *The Future of Children* 26(2): 139–158.

Sciaraffa, Mary, Paula Zeanah, and Charles Zeanah. 2018. "Understanding and Promoting Resilience in the Context of Adverse Childhood Experiences." *Early Childhood Education Journal* 46(3): 343–353.

Sparks, Sarah. 2017. "How Teachers' Stress Affects Students: A Research Roundup." Education Week. https://www.edweek.org/tm/articles/2017/06/07/how-teachers-stress-affects-students-a-research.html

Stein, Amanda, et al. 2013. "The Educare Chicago Research-Program Partnership and Follow-Up Study: Using Data on Program Graduates to Enhance Quality Improvement Efforts." *Early Education and Development* 24(1): 19–41.

Stoltz, Dorothy, et al. 2015. "Just Good Practice: Engaging Families with Young Children." *Public Libraries* 54(5): 27–30.

Van Voorhis, Frances, Michelle Maier, Joyce Epstein, and Chrishana Lloyd. 2013. *The Impact of Family Involvement on the Education of Children Ages 3 to 9*. New York, NY: MDRC.

Virmani, Elita Amini, Ann-Marie Wiese, and Peter Mangione. 2016. "Pathways to Relational Family Engagement with Culturally and Linguistically Diverse Families: Can Reflective Practice Guide Us?" In *Family Involvement in Early Education and Child Care,* vol. 20 of Advances in Early Education and Day Care. Bingley, UK: Emerald Group Publishing.

Whitaker, Robert, Tracy Dearth-Wesley, and Rachel Gooze. 2015. "Workplace Stress and the Quality of Teacher-Children Relationships in Head Start." *Early Childhood Research Quarterly* 30(1): 57–69.

WIDA. 2017. *WIDA Early Years Guiding Principles of Language Development.* Madison, WI: Board of Regents of the University of Wisconsin System. https://wida.wisc.edu/sites/default/files/resource/Guiding-Principles-of-Early-ELD.pdf

Wright, Travis, and Sharon Ryan. 2014. "Toddlers through Primary Grades: Too Scared to Learn: Teaching Young Children Who Have Experienced Trauma." *Young Children* 69(5): 88–93.

Chapter 7

Allensworth, Elaine, Stephen Ponisciak, and Christopher Mazzeo. 2009. *The Schools Teachers Leave: Teacher Mobility in Chicago Public Schools.* Chicago, IL: Consortium on Chicago School Research at the University of Chicago. https://consortium.uchicago.edu/sites/default/files/2018-10/CCSR_Teacher_Mobility.pdf

Blank, Helen. 1997. "Advocacy Leadership." In *Leadership in Early Care and Education.* Sharon Kagan and Barbara Bowman, eds. Washington, DC: NAEYC.

Bloom, Paula Jorde. 2000. "Images from the Field: How Directors View Their Organizations, Their Roles, and Their Jobs." In *Managing Quality in Young Children's Programs: The Leader's Role.* New York, NY: Teachers College Press.

Bloom, Paula Jorde. 2015. *Blueprint for Action: Leading your Team in Continuous Quality Improvement.* 3rd ed. Lake Forest, IL: New Horizons.

Bloom, Paula Jorde. 2016. *Measuring Work Attitudes in the Early Childhood Setting: Technical Manual for the Early Childhood Job Satisfaction Survey and Early Childhood Work Environment Survey.* 3rd ed. Wheeling, IL: McCormick Center for Early Childhood Leadership, National Louis University.

Bloom, Paula Jorde, Ann Hentschel, and Jill Bella. 2010. *A Great Place to Work: Creating a Healthy Organizational Climate.* Lake Forest, IL: New Horizons.

Bloom, Paula Jorde, Safiyah Jackson, Teri Talan, and Robyn Kelton. 2013. *Taking Charge of Change: A 20-Year Review of Empowering Early Childhood Administrators through Leadership Training.* Wheeling, IL: McCormick Center for Early Childhood Leadership, National Louis University. https://mccormick-assets.floodlight.design/wp-content/uploads/2018/03/tcc20report.pdf

Crompton, Dwayne. 1997. "Community Leadership." In *Leadership in Early Care and Education.* Sharon Kagan and Barbara Bowman, eds. Washington, DC: NAEYC.

Dennis, Sarah, and Erin O'Connor. 2013. "Reexamining Quality in Early Childhood Education: Exploring the Relationship between the Organizational Climate and the Classroom." *Journal of Research in Childhood Education* 27(1): 74–92.

Douglass, Anne. 2017. *Leading for Change in Early Care and Education: Cultivating Leadership from Within.* New York, NY: Teachers College Press.

Institute of Medicine, and National Research Council. 2015. *Transforming the Workforce for Children Birth through Age 8: A Unifying Foundation*. Washington, DC: The National Academies Press. https://www.fcd-us.org/assets/2016/10/IOMNRCFullReport2015.pdf

Kagan, Sharon Lynn, et al. 2008. *New York City Early Care and Education Unified Performance Measurement System: A Pilot Study*. New York, NY: National Center for Children and Families.

Kania, John, and Mark Kramer. 2011. "Embracing Emergence: How Collective Impact Addresses Complexity." *Stanford Social Innovation Review*. https://ssir.org/articles/entry/collective_impact

Lower, Joanna, and Deborah Cassidy. 2007. "Child Care Work Environments: The Relationship with Learning Environments." *Journal of Research in Childhood Education* 22(2): 189–204.

Maurer, Robert. 2013. *The Spirit of Kaizen: Creating Lasting Excellence One Step at a Time*. New York, NY: McGraw-Hill.

McCormick Center for Early Childhood Leadership. 2010. "Head Start Administrative Practices, Director Qualifications, and Links to Classroom Quality." Wheeling, IL: McCormick Center for Early Childhood Leadership Publications. https://digitalcommons.nl.edu/mccormickcenter-pubs/20/

O'Neill, Cassandra, and Monica Brinkerhoff. 2017. *Five Elements of Collective Leadership for Early Childhood Professionals*. St. Paul, MN, and Washington, DC: Redleaf Press and NAEYC.

Porter, Noriko. 2012. "High Turnover among Early Childhood Educators in the United States." Child Research Net. https://www.childresearch.net/projects/ecec/2012_04.html

Talan, Teri, and Paula Jorde Bloom. 2011. *Program Administration Scale: Measuring Early Childhood Leadership and Management*. 2nd ed. New York, NY: Teachers College Press.

Talan, Teri, Paula Jorde Bloom, and Robyn Kelton. 2014. "Building the Leadership Capacity of Early Childhood Directors: An Evaluation of a Leadership Development Model." *Early Childhood Research and Practice* 16(1 and 2): n.p. http://ecrp.uiuc.edu/v16n1/talan.html

Whitebook, Marcy, Deborah Phillips, and Carollee Howes. 2014. *Worthy Work, STILL Unlivable Wages: The Early Childhood Workforce 25 Years after the National Child Care Staffing Study*. Berkeley, CA: Center for the Study of Child Care Employment, University of California. http://cscce.berkeley.edu/files/2014/ReportFINAL.pdf

Whitehead, Joellyn, Kevin Anderson, Johnna Darragh Ernst, and Deborah Presley. 2016. "Illinois Salary and Staffing Survey of Licensed Child Care Facilities: Fiscal Year 2015." Illinois Department of Health and Human Services. http://www.dhs.state.il.us/page.aspx?item=85484

W. K. Kellogg Foundation. 2007. *The Collective Leadership Framework: A Workbook for Cultivating and Sustaining Community Change*. Battle Creek, MI: W. K. Kellogg Foundation. http://go-neighborhoods.org/wp-content/go_neigh_pdfs/Tool_Box/5_Successfully_Work_with_Others/document_Collective%20Leadership%20-%20Kellogg.pdf

Young, Billie. 2017. *Continuous Quality Improvement in Early Childhood and School Age Programs: An Update from the Field*. Boston, MA: Build Initiative. https://qrisnetwork.org/sites/all/files/session/resources/Continuous%20Quality%20Improvement%20in%20Early%20Childhood%20and%20School%20Age%20Programs%20-%20An%20Update%20from%20the%20Field.pdf

Chapter 8

Abel, Mike, Teri Talan, and Marie Masterson. 2017. "Whole Leadership: A Framework for Early Childhood Programs." *Exchange* 39(233): 22–25.

Ackerman, Debra J. 2008. "Coaching as Part of a Pilot Quality Rating Scale Initiative: Challenges to— and Supports for—the Change-Making Process." *Early Childhood Research and Practice* 10(2): n.p. http://ecrp.uiuc.edu/v10n2/ackerman.html

Ackerman, Debra J., and Rachel A. Sansanelli. 2010. "The Source of Child Care Center Preschool Learning and Program Standards: Implications for Potential Early Learning Challenge Fund Grantees." *Early Childhood Research and Practice* 12(2): n.p. http://ecrp.uiuc.edu/v12n1/ ackerman.html

Bloom, Paula Jorde. 2011. *Circle of Influence: Implementing Shared Decision Making and Participative Management*. 2nd ed. Lake Forest, IL: New Horizons.

Bloom, Paula Jorde, Ann Hentschel, and Jill Bella. 2013. *Inspiring Peak Performance: Competence, Commitment, and Collaboration*. Lake Forest, IL: New Horizons.

Brynteson, Richard. 2006. *Once upon a Complex Time: Using Stories to Understand Systems*. Farmington, MN: Sparrow Media Group.

Cooperrider, David, and Suresh Srivastva. 2017. "The Gift of New Eyes: Personal Reflections after Thirty Years of Appreciative Inquiry in Organizational Life." In *Research in Organizational Change and Development*, vol. 25 of Research in Organizational Change and Development. Bingley, UK: Emerald Publishing.

Dennis, Sarah, and Erin O'Connor. 2013. "Reexamining Quality in Early Childhood Education: Exploring the Relationship between the Organizational Climate and the Classroom." *Journal of Research in Childhood Education* 27(1): 74–92.

Douglass, Anne. 2017. *Leading for Change in Early Care and Education: Cultivating Leadership from Within*. New York, NY: Teachers College Press.

Haines, Stephen G. 2000. *The Complete Guide to Systems Thinking and Learning*. Amherst, MA: HRD Press.

Hammond, Sue Annis. 2013. *The Thin Book of Appreciative Inquiry*. 3rd ed. Bend, OR: Thin Book Publishing.

Jiang, Hua, and Rita Linjuan Men. 2017. "Creating an Engaged Workforce: The Impact of Authentic Leadership, Transparent Organizational Communication, and Work-Life Enrichment." *Communication Research* 44(2): 225–243.

Long, Susi, Mariana Souto-Manning, and Vivian Maria Vasquez. 2016. *Courageous Leadership in Early Childhood Education: Taking a Stand for Social Justice*. New York, NY: Teachers College Press.

Lower, Joanna, and Deborah Cassidy. 2007. "Child Care Work Environments: The Relationship with Learning Environments." *Journal of Research in Childhood Education* 22(2): 189–204.

Mims, Sharon U., et al. 2008. "Education Level and Stability as It Relates to Early Childhood Classroom Quality: A Survey of Early Childhood Program Directors and Teachers." *Journal of Research in Childhood Education* 23(2): 227–237.

NAEYC. 2018. *NAEYC Early Learning Program Accreditation Standards and Assessment Items*. Washington, DC: NAEYC. https://www.naeyc.org/sites/default/files/globally-shared/ downloads/PDFs/accreditation/early-learning/standards_and_assessment_web_1.pdf

Page, Ana, Monica Brinkerhoff, Mary Beth Salomone Testa, and Samantha Marshall. 2016. "Advocacy: From Awareness to Action." *Exchange* 229(May/June): 23–26.

Rohacek, Monica, et al. 2010. *Understanding Quality in Context: Child Care Centers, Communities, Markets, and Public Policy*. Washington, DC: Urban Institute. https://www.urban.org/sites/default/files/publication/29051/412191-Understanding-Quality-in-Context-Child-Care-Centers-Communities-Markets-and-Public-Policy.PDF

Senge, Peter. 1990. *The Fifth Discipline: The Art and Practice of the Learning Organization*. New York, NY: Doubleday/Currency.

Spillane, James P. 2006. *Distributed Leadership*. San Francisco, CA: John Wiley and Sons.

Talan, Teri. 2010. "Distributed Leadership: Something New or Something Borrowed?" *Exchange* 193(May/June): 8–10.

Talan, Teri, and Paula Jorde Bloom. 2011. *Program Administration Scale: Measuring Early Childhood Leadership and Management*. 2nd ed. New York, NY: Teachers College Press.

Totenhagen, Casey, et al. 2016. "Retaining Early Childhood Education Workers: A Review of the Empirical Literature." *Journal of Research in Childhood Education* 30(4): 585–599.

Wells, Michael B. 2015. "Predicting Preschool Teacher Retention and Turnover in Newly Hired Head Start Teachers across the First Half of the School Year." *Early Childhood Research Quarterly* 30A(1): 152–159.

Chapter 9

Bloom, Paula Jorde. 2016. *Measuring Work Attitudes in the Early Childhood Setting: Technical Manual for the Early Childhood Job Satisfaction Survey and Early Childhood Work Environment Survey*. 3rd ed. Wheeling, IL: National Louis University, McCormick Center for Early Childhood Leadership.

Bloom, Paula Jorde, and Michael Abel. 2015. "Expanding the Lens: Leadership as an Organizational Asset." *Young Children* 70(2): 10–17.

Campion, Linda. 2018. "Leadership Styles: Considering Context and Climate." *TechTrends* 62(4): 412–413.

Dennis, Sarah, and Erin O'Connor. 2013. "Reexamining Quality in Early Childhood Education: Exploring the Relationship between the Organizational Climate and the Classroom." *Journal of Research in Childhood Education* 27(1): 74–92.

Doherty, Gillian, Tammy McCormick Ferguson, Glory Ressler, and Jonathan Lomotey. 2015. "Enhancing Child Care Quality by Director Training and Collegial Mentoring." *Early Childhood Research and Practice* 17(1): n.p. http://ecrp.uiuc.edu/v17n1/doherty.html

Guo, Ying, et al. 2011. "Preschool Teachers' Sense of Community, Instructional Quality, and Children's Language and Literacy Gains." *Early Education and Development* 22(2): 206–233.

Hamre, Bridget, Bridget Hatfield, Robert Pianta, and Jamil Faiza. 2014. "Evidence for General and Domain-Specific Elements of Teacher-Child Interactions: Associations with Preschool Children's Development." *Child Development* 85(3): 1257–1274.

Isaksen, Scott II, and Hans Akkermans. 2011. "Creative Climate: A Leadership Lever for Innovation." *Journal of Creative Behavior* 45(3): 161–187.

Jaruszewicz, Candace, and Mary White. 2009. "The Teachergarten: Creating an Environment Conducive to Meaningful Teacher Growth." *Early Childhood Education Journal* 37(3): 171–174.

Jeon, Lieny, Cynthia Buettner, and Ashley Grant. 2018. "Early Childhood Teachers' Psychological Well-Being: Exploring Potential Predictors of Depression, Stress, and Emotional Exhaustion." *Early Education and Development* 29(1): 53–69.

Masterson, Marie, and Katharine Kersey. 2013 "Connecting Children to Kindness: Encouraging a Culture of Empathy." *Childhood Education* 89(4): 211–216.

McGinty, Anita, Laura Justice, and Sara Rimm-Kaufman. 2008. "Sense of School Community for Preschool Teachers Serving At-Risk Children." *Early Education and Development* 19(2): 361–384.

Neugebauer, Roger. 2016. "Standing Up and Being Heard: The Director's Other Job." *Exchange* 229(May/June): 27–29.

Page, Ana, Monica Brinkerhoff, Mary Beth Salomone Testa, and Samantha Marshall. 2016. "Advocacy: From Awareness to Action." *Exchange* 229(May/June): 23–26.

Pianta, Robert, Jason Downer, and Bridget Hamre. 2016. "Quality in Early Education Classrooms: Definitions, Gaps, and Systems." *The Future of Children* 26(2): 119–137.

Toytok, Esef Hakan, and Saduman Kapusuzoglu. 2015. "Influence of School Managers' Ethical Leadership Behaviors on Organizational Culture: Teachers' Perceptions." *Eurasian Journal of Educational Research* 66: 373–388.

Wanless, Shannon. 2016. "The Role of Psychological Safety in Human Development." *Research in Human Development* 13(1): 6–14.

Wanless, Shannon, and Dana Winters. 2018. "A Welcome Space for Taking Risks: Psychological Safety Creates a Positive Climate for Learning." *Learning Professional* 39(4): 41–44.

Index

A

Abuse. See Trauma-informed teaching

Active listening, 38, 73, 104

Active play, 84

Adaptability, 16–17, 30–35, 56

    defined, 27

Administrative leadership, 1, 7–8, 10, 57, 92, 98, 146

    advancing, 107–120

    advocacy leadership, 116, 126–127

    best practices, 109, 112, 115–116, 123, 129

    community leadership, 127

    connecting with pedagogical leadership, 112

    consensus building, 125

    defined, 2–3

    exploring, 119–120

    goal setting, 111–113

    integrating priorities, 123

    operational leadership, 108–110, 122–123

    operational leadership, 130–131

    putting into practice, 130–131

    resources, 128

    retaining staff, 109

    strategic leadership, 111–113, 124–125

    strengthening community partnerships, 116–117

    tools for, 121–131

    understanding, 113–115

    vs. management, 117–118

Adult learning, 58

    principles of, 86–87

Advocacy leadership, 3, 107, 119, 126–127, 140–141

    building, 116–118

    understanding, 113–115

Anti-Discrimination Position Statement (NAEYC), 60

Appreciative inquiry, 122

Assessment, 58

    bias-free, 85–86

    children's development and learning, 67–68

Asynchronistic development, 103

Authenticity, 16–17, 23–24, 30–35, 56, 60

B

Balancing priorities, 1, 7, 24

Beliefs about how children learn, 61–62

Bias-free curriculum, 85–86

Brainstorming, 18, 22, 109

Budgets, 2, 129, 138

BUILD Initiative, 141

Building consensus, 16–17

C

Center on the Social and Emotional Foundations for Early Learning, 84

Centers for Disease Control and Prevention, 9, 68

Child Care Bureau, 84

Child protective services, 44–47

Child Trends, 100

Child-development theory, 58

    applying, 79–80

Classroom Assessment Scoring System at Teachstone, 74

Coaching, 52, 58

    building skills, 87–90

Cocaring framework, 102–104

Code of Ethical Conduct (NAEYC), 45

Cognitive development, 9–10, 52, 83

Collaboration, 1, 5–6, 8, 17, 19, 22–23, 26, 52, 122, 127

Communication, 2, 17, 22, 36–39, 96, 98
    inviting, 136–137
Communities of practice, 2, 52–53
Community leadership, 3, 8, 107, 116–119
    developing, 127–129
Community partnerships, 135–136, 146
Conflict, 6, 42, 52
Consensus building, 125–127
Consistency, 58
Consultation, 52
Continuous quality improvement, 112, 133–134
Coordinated models of care, 102–104
Creativity, 16–17, 21–23, 30–35, 56, 138
Critical thinking, 22
Cultural competence, 17, 36, 43–44
Culturally responsive practice, 8, 10, 51, 76
    curriculum and assessment, 85–86
    ensuring, 95–97
Curriculum
    bias-free, 85–86
    development, 57
    impact of, 62–63
    review, 81
    role of pedagogical leader, 77–78
    sample, 82

D
Developing talent, 123
Developmentally appropriate practice, 8, 10, 60
    zone of proximal development, 64
Distributed leadership, 62
Dual language learners, 94
    supporting, 97–99

E
Early Childhood Technical Assistance Center, 84

Early Childhood Work Environment Survey, 8, 109
Early English Language Development Standards (WIDA), 99
Early Years Guiding Principles of Language Development (WIDA), 99
Empathy, 16–17, 20–21, 30–35, 56
    defined, 20
Entrepreneurial focus, 125
Ethical conduct, 17, 36, 44–46
Evaluation, 8, 58
Evidence-based teaching, 58, 82–84
Executive function, 72, 84

F
Family engagement, 3, 5, 8–11, 23, 58
    assessing, 105–106
    best practices, 94–95, 99, 101
    building on strengths, 64–66
    connecting families with resources, 140–141
    coordinated models of care, 102–104
    culturally responsive, 43–44, 51, 66, 76, 95–99
    encouraging, 93–106
    evaluating, 70
    resources, 99–100
    strengthening resilience, 101–102
    supporting dual language learners, 97–99
    trauma-informed teaching, 99–101
Feedback, 2, 16, 18, 42, 49
Financial knowledge, 123
Fostering insight, 39
Frank Porter Graham (FPG) Child Development Institute, 99
Funding, 2

G
Goal setting, 111–113
Growth mindset, 27

H

High-quality interactions, 74

Horizontal continuity, 103

Humility, 16–17, 25–26, 30–35, 56, 96

I

Implementation science, 81

Innovation, 22

Instructional leadership, 3, 58, 62

Intentionality, 17, 36, 46–48, 56

Interdependence, 147

L

Language development, 9–10, 52, 60, 71, 83, 94

Leadership

administrative, 1–3, 7–8, 10, 57, 92, 107–131

adopting the Whole Leadership Framework, 145–149

advocacy, 3, 107, 113–119, 126–127, 140–141

aiming for excellence, 10–11

anchoring your work, 7

best practices, 6, 8, 10, 134, 138

community partnerships and resources, 135–136, 146

community, 3, 8, 107, 116–119, 127–129

connecting families with resources, 140–141

continuous quality improvement, 133–134

developing a purpose statement, 12

distributed, 62

exploring influence, 13–15

fostering effective learning, 135

increasing your impact, 142–143

instructional, 3, 58, 62

inviting communication, 136–137

leveraging your qualities, 132–149

maximizing human capacity, 137–139

operational, 2–3, 107–110, 119, 122–123, 130–131

pedagogical, 1–3, 7, 58–92, 112

positive culture, 137–139

reflection, 143–144

resources, 141

strategic, 3, 107, 111–113, 119, 124–125

time management, 5–8

trauma-informed care, 9

understanding the impact, 138

understanding your influence, 5–15

vision and practice, 6, 11–12

vs. management, 117–118

whole-child mindset, 9

Leadership essentials, 1, 16–35, 91–92, 130–131, 146

adaptability, 16, 27, 30–35

applying, 30

authenticity, 16, 23–24, 30–35

balancing responsibilities, 24

best practices, 19, 21–22, 24–25, 42, 44, 51

communication, 36–39

creativity, 16, 21–23, 30–35

cultural competence, 36, 43–44

defined, 2–3

elements of, 17

empathy, 16, 20–21, 30–35

engaging staff, 49

ethical conduct, 36, 44–46

exploring, 31–35

fostering insight, 39

humility, 16, 25–26

inspiring respect, 37

intentionality, 36, 46–47

management skills, 36, 48–49

morality, 36, 44–46

motivating people, 36, 48–49

ongoing learning, 16, 28–29, 30–35

pedagogy, 50

professionalism, 36, 51–53

putting into practice, 55–57

reflection, 42

resources, 54

self-appraisal, 42

self-awareness, 36, 40–41

self-efficacy, 16, 18–19, 30–35

team building, 36–39

tools, 36–57

transparency, 16–17, 23–24, 30–35

using change, 28

Learning

adults, 58, 86–87

beliefs about children, 61–62

fostering effective, 135

ongoing, 16–17, 28–29, 30–35, 51–52, 56

Learning environment, 2, 58

optimizing, 70–71

Legal knowledge, 123

Literacy development, 83, 94

M

Maintaining norms, 8

Management skills, 17, 36, 48–49

vs. leadership, 117–118

Marketing, 124–125

Maximizing human capacity, 137–139

McCormick Center for Early Childhood Leadership, 1, 29, 54, 109, 141

Measuring progress, 10–11

Mentoring, 52–53, 58

building skills, 87–90

Milestone Tracker (CDC), 68

Morality, 17, 36, 44–46

Motivating people, 17, 36, 48–49, 72–73

N

NAEYC Early Learning Program Accreditation Standards and Assessment Items, 128

National Association for Family Child Care, 141

National Association for the Education of Young Children (NAEYC), 45–46, 60, 67, 95, 141

Accreditation Standard 2–Curriculum, 82

Accreditation Standard 10–Leadership and Management, 128

National Center for Children in Poverty Young Child Risk Calculator, 100

National Child Traumatic Stress Network, 100

National Research Council, 1, 103

National Scientific Council on the Developing Child, 99–100

O

Observation to inform teaching, 68–70

Ongoing learning, 16–17, 28–29, 30–35, 51–52, 56

Operational leadership, 2–3, 107, 119, 130–131

maximizing, 122–123

Organizational climate, 110

P

Pedagogical leadership, 1, 7, 10, 50, 57, 130–131, 146

adult learning principles, 79, 86–87

and administrative leadership, 98, 112

art and science of teaching, 58–60, 74–75

assessing learning, 67–70

beliefs about how children learn, 61–62

best practices, 60, 62, 64, 66, 72, 81, 83–84

bias-free curriculum and assessment, 85–86

child-development theory and research, 79–80

coaching and mentoring, 79, 87–90

components, 58

curricular development, 77–78

defined, 2–3

developmentally appropriate practice, 60

distributed leadership, 62

evidence-based teaching, 79, 82–84

exploring, 75–78

family engagement, 64–66, 76

high-quality interactions, 74

impact of curriculum, 62–63

learning environment, 58, 70–71

maximizing, 58–78

motivating staff, 72–73

observation, 68

putting into practice, 91–92

resources, 82, 84

responsive teaching, 64

technical credibility, 79, 89–90

tools for, 79–92

understanding executive function, 72

using implementation science, 81

zone of proximal development, 64

Persistence, 73

Physical development, 52

Plan, Do, Study, Act strategy, 112

Positive culture, 137–139

Preliteracy skills, 10

Problem solving, 22, 38, 52, 64, 73, 123

Professional development, 2, 51–52, 122–123

Professional learning communities, 79–80

Professionalism, 36, 51–53

Program Administration Scale, 128, 145

Program philosophy, 2, 7

Public relations, 124–125

Purpose statements, 12

Q

QRIS National Learning Network, 54

R

Reflective practice, 29, 143–144

Reggio Emilia, 61, 108

Relationship building, 2

Resilience, 101–104

Resources

bias-free programs, 86

connecting families and children with, 140–141

embracing advocacy, 141

evidence-based curriculum, 84

exploring high-quality interactions, 74

improving administrative leadership, 126, 128

NAEYC Accreditation Standard 2–Curriculum, 82

resources for growth, 54

supporting dual language learners, 99

trauma-informed care, 9

Respect, 37

Responsive teaching, 64

Retaining staff, 109–110

Routines, 2, 16, 16

S

Scaffolding, 64, 66, 83, 87, 101

Selecting curriculum, 2

Self-awareness, 2, 17, 36, 40–41

Self-efficacy, 16–17, 18–19, 30–35, 56, 84, 101

Self-reflection, 40–42, 56

Self-regulation, 40, 71–73, 83–84

Setting goals, 10–11, 19

Sheltered Instruction Observation Protocol, 99

Social capital, 21–23

Social-emotional development, 9–10, 52, 73, 83

Special needs, 94, 96

Staff turnover, 109–110

State guidelines, 54

Strategic leadership, 3, 107, 119
    inspiring, 111–113
    maximizing, 124–125
Stress management, 83
Study guides
    adopting the Whole Leadership Framework, 145–149
    assessing family engagement, 105–106
    exploring administrative leadership, 119–120
    exploring influence, 13–15
    exploring leadership essentials, 31–35
    exploring pedagogical leadership, 75–79
    putting administrative leadership into practice, 130–131
    putting leadership essentials into practice, 55–57
    putting pedagogical leadership into practice, 91–92
Synergy, 117–118
Systems thinking, 123

T

Teacher qualifications, 2
Teaching, 2
    art and science of, 58–60, 75–76
    evidence-based, 82–84
Team building, 36–39, 55
Technical credibility, 58, 60, 79, 89–90
Time logs, 6
Time management, 5–8, 47–48
Transparency, 16–17, 23–24, 30–35, 56, 60, 122
Trauma-informed teaching, 9, 99–101
Trust, 122

U

U.S. Department of Education, 99
U.S. Department of Health and Human Services Administration for Children and Families, 9, 99

Unintended consequences, 148

V

Vertical continuity, 103
Vulnerable children, 71

W

Whole Leadership Framework, 132–149
    adopting, 145–149
    best practices, 134, 138
    community partnerships and resources, 135–136, 146
    connecting families with resources, 140–141
    continuous quality improvement, 133–134
    defined, 2–3
    fostering effective learning, 135
    increasing your impact, 142–143
    inviting communication, 136–137
    maximizing human capacity, 137–139
    origins, 1
    positive culture, 137–139
    reflection, 143–144
    resources, 141
Whole-child mindset, 9–11
Workshops, 52

Z

Zone of proximal development, 64